1

Contents

Acknowledgement

First and foremost, I want to express my deepest gratitude to you, dear reader. Without you, "L.I.F.E. - Legacy in Forming Excellence" would remain a dream. Your support and encouragement have been the wind beneath my wings, propelling me on this incredible journey.

I am immensely grateful to my family, whose unwavering belief in my vision has been a beacon of light in times of doubt. Your love and support have been my strength and my inspiration. I would like to express my deepest gratitude to those who have made this journey possible. To my mother, whose goal-oriented approach has been a guiding light in my life, teaching me the importance of setting objectives and relentlessly pursuing them. To my father, who has shown me the beauty of simplicity and the satisfaction that comes from wanting less. To Ami Di, whose unwavering support throughout my book writing journey has been a pillar of strength. To Grishmy, my critic reviewer, whose constructive feedback has always pushed me to strive for better. To Vishal Jiju, whose motivational spirit has been a driving force behind my endeavors. And last but certainly not least, my most special thanks to my all-time companion, my niece Vidhi, whose presence has added immeasurable joy to my life.

A special thanks to **Aashish Sethna**, my first mentor and guide, who instilled in me the confidence to dream big. To **Madhavi Mam**, **Mahesh Dubey Sir**, and **Tarapada Dutta Sir**, thank you for forming my roots strong and guiding me in my journey. Thank you, **Sunita mam**, to always be besides me motivating to write and supporting in all possible ways.

To my wonderful team who have supported me in all possible ways, I am forever grateful. **Rony**, for your exceptional work in designing the book cover, **Smita**, for your meticulous proof-reading, and **Vivek, Geeta, Nimisha, and Annuradha**, for motivating me and helping me focus clear by taking all work responsibilities, I extend my heartfelt thanks.

To my friends, **Bhavesh Koriya**, who always guided me about learnings from nature, **Sanket Kharsambale and Archana Sand,** who indirectly always supported me with healthy talks and shared learnings. Your friendship has been a source of strength and inspiration.

"L.I.F.E. - Legacy in Forming Excellence" is a testament to the collective efforts of many. It is a book born out of love, nurtured with passion, and brought to life by a community. This book is a testament to all of you, and for that, I am eternally grateful. Thank you, one and all, for being a part of this journey.

Author's Review by Sunita Bansdawala

In the grand symphony of existence, where each life is a verse in a cosmic ballad, there emerges a storyteller whose words paint portraits of resilience, compassion, and the relentless pursuit of meaning. Sumi Ajmera, who has learnt how to be a weaver of tales, has her pen dancing across the page like a maestro conducting an orchestra. As I reflect upon the rich tapestry she has woven in the entire book, yet chapter 4 creates a lasting impression on me, "Life Milestones and Turning Points."

In this 4th chapter, I am reminded of the power of storytelling—the ability to illuminate the ordinary moments and transform them into extraordinary journeys. Sumi Ajmera's words are not merely ink on paper; they are brushstrokes on the canvas of our souls, inviting us to embark on a voyage of self-discovery and transformation. In this chapter, she delves deep into the nuances of life's milestones, turning points, and quiet revolutions, each word a guiding star illuminating the path towards individual growth and authenticity.

As I traverse the landscapes of Sumi's prose, I am struck by three major aspects that resonate deeply within me:

- Firstly, Sumi celebrates the mosaic of moments that shape our existence, reminding us that life is not just a series of grand events, but memories woven from the threads of everyday experiences. Like a skilled artist, she encourages us to embrace the beauty of the mundane, finding solace and purpose in the seemingly ordinary moments that often become unnoticed.

- Secondly, Sumi explores the transformative power of self-discovery, urging us to listen to the whispers of our inner selves and embark on a journey of introspection and growth. Through the stories of Nicolae, Emma, Rajiv, Sarah, and Mark, she illustrates the profound impact that mindfulness, reflection, and unplugged adventures can have on our lives, guiding us toward a deeper understanding of ourselves and the world around us.

- And finally, Sumi reminds us of the fragility of time and the importance of cherishing each moment as a precious gift. Like a gentle breeze stirring the leaves of a tree, her words prompt us to pause, breathe, and immerse ourselves fully in the richness of life, knowing that every tick of the clock is an opportunity to create memorable memories, bond with connections, and leave a legacy that transcends the boundaries of time itself.

Dear Sumi, your words are more than just stories to me and your readers; they are beacons of hope, wisdom, and inspiration lighting the way for all who seek meaning and purpose in this wonderful journey called 'L.I.F.E'. As I dedicate this foreword to you, I am filled with gratitude for the gift of your storytelling and the profound impact it has had on my own life. May your words continue to touch hearts, ignite minds, and illuminate the path toward a brighter, more compassionate world!

With warmest regards,

Sunita Bansdawala
[AUTHORPRENEUR]

Preface

Hello, dear reader! Welcome to a journey, an adventure, a celebration of life itself. Welcome to "L.I.F.E. - Legacy in Forming Excellence". This book is a labor of love, a tribute to the human spirit, and a testament to the power of striving for excellence.

"L.I.F.E." stands for Legacy in Forming Excellence, and that's exactly what this book is all about. It's about the footprints we leave in the sands of time, the echoes of our actions that reverberate through the ages. It's about striving for the best, pushing our boundaries, and reaching for the stars.

As you turn the pages of this book, you'll meet extraordinary individuals who have left an indelible mark on the world. You'll discover the transformative power of perseverance, the beauty of resilience, and the triumph of the human spirit. You'll learn about the magic that happens when we strive for excellence and the legacy that such a pursuit leaves behind.

But this book is more than just a collection of stories and lessons. It's a friend, a mentor, a source of inspiration. It's a beacon of light guiding you on your journey towards excellence. It's a call to action, urging you to create a legacy that resonates with your highest ideals.

So, dear reader, as you embark on this journey through the pages of "L.I.F.E. - Legacy in Forming Excellence", I hope you find inspiration, wisdom, and a renewed sense of purpose. May this book be your companion on your journey towards excellence, and may it inspire you to leave a legacy that shines brightly in the tapestry of life.

Welcome aboard, dear friend. Let's embark on this exciting journey together. Welcome to "L.I.F.E. - Legacy in Forming Excellence".

Chapter 1: L.I.F.E.

Legacy In Forming Excellence

Remember our banyan tree? Legacy, my friend, is its shade—the cool refuge where weary souls rest, where stories intertwine, and where the echo of our laughter lingers. Let's weave this tale of legacy and excellence using the gentle threads of proverbs and similes, like a banyan tree's intricate roots embracing the earth.

Roots of Foundation: The banyan tree, like a legacy, begins as a humble seed. Yet, over time, its roots delve deep into the earth, intertwining with the soil and drawing sustenance. These roots symbolize the foundations upon which greatness is built. Just as the banyan's roots provide stability, a legacy rest upon values, principles, and wisdom passed down through generations. These roots anchor excellence, nourishing it even during storms.

Branches of Influence: Imagine the sprawling branches of a mature banyan tree, stretching out in all directions. Similarly, a legacy extends far beyond individual achievements. It reaches across time and space, touching lives, inspiring hearts, and shaping destinies. Leaders, teachers, and visionaries leave behind branches of influence—lessons learned, innovations shared, and wisdom imparted. These branches continue to thrive, casting their shade upon generations yet unborn.

Adaptability and Growth: Banyan trees are masters of adaptation. They send down aerial roots that eventually become new trunks, forming a network of interconnected growth. Likewise, a legacy evolves. It embraces change, learns from setbacks, and adapts to new challenges. Excellence is not static; it grows, much like the banyan's ever-expanding canopy. Each setback becomes a stepping stone, and every change an opportunity for growth.

Shelter and Support: Under the banyan's shade, communities gather—a refuge from the scorching sun. Similarly, a legacy provides shelter. It is a safe space where knowledge, creativity, and innovation flourish. Like the banyan's protective canopy, a legacy supports those who aspire to achieve greatness. It nurtures their potential, shielding them from adversity and encouraging them to reach for the sky.

Timelessness: Banyan trees endure across centuries. Their presence transcends epochs, witnessing the rise and fall of civilizations. Similarly, a legacy outlasts individuals. It leaves an indelible mark on history, shaping cultures, inspiring revolutions, and defining eras. Excellence becomes timeless—a beacon for future generations.

In the quiet strength of a banyan tree, we find the essence of legacy—a testament to the pursuit of excellence that shapes our world. So let us plant our seeds, nurture our roots, and let our branches touch the sky. For in this dance of life, we become the banyans of our own legacy.

The Sculptor's Legacy: Once upon a time, in the small town of Artisia, lived a renowned sculptor named Aristo. He was known for his exquisite sculptures that were so lifelike, they were often mistaken for real people. Aristo had a son, Elio, who was keen on following his father's footsteps. Aristo believed in the mantra, "Legacy In Forming Excellence". He taught Elio that every stroke of their chisel on the marble was not just about creating a sculpture, but about leaving a legacy of excellence. Elio, inspired by his father's words, worked diligently, honing his skills. Years later, when Aristo passed away, Elio took up his father's mantle. His sculptures were as lifelike as his father's, if not more. The town of Artisia continued to be known for its excellent sculptures, and Aristo's legacy lived on through Elio's work.

The Chef's Excellence: In the bustling city of Gourmetville, Chef Gustavo ran a small but popular restaurant. Gustavo was famous for his unique and delicious recipes. His daughter, Bella, grew up watching her father create culinary masterpieces. Gustavo always told Bella, "Our legacy lies in forming excellence. It's not just about cooking food, it's about crafting an experience." Inspired, Bella decided to learn the art of cooking from her father. When Gustavo retired, Bella took over the restaurant. She introduced new dishes while keeping her father's classics on the menu. The restaurant's popularity soared, and Bella's culinary excellence became the talk of the town. Through Bella's dishes, Gustavo's legacy of excellence continued to thrive.

The Legacy of the Lighthouse Keeper: In the coastal town of Beacon's Edge, there was a lighthouse that had been maintained by the same family for generations. The current keeper, Old Tom, was a descendant of the original lighthouse keeper. Tom was known throughout the town for his dedication to keeping the lighthouse functioning, ensuring the safety of ships passing by the rocky coast. Tom had a grandson, Young Tim, who was fascinated by the lighthouse. Tom would often tell Tim, "Our family's legacy is this lighthouse. We form excellence by ensuring its light never goes out." Inspired by his grandfather's words, Tim learned everything about the lighthouse. When Old Tom passed away, Young Tim took over the duties of the lighthouse keeper. He maintained the lighthouse with the same dedication as his grandfather. The legacy of excellence continued, and the lighthouse at Beacon's Edge remained a beacon of safety for all.

The Legacy of the Librarian: In the city of Litera, there was a library known for its vast collection of books. The librarian, Miss Penelope, was an elderly woman who had dedicated her life to the preservation and expansion of the library's collection. Penelope had a niece, Sophia, who loved spending time in the library. Penelope would often tell Sophia, "Our legacy is in forming excellence through knowledge. Each book in this library is a testament to that legacy." Inspired by her aunt, Sophia decided to become a librarian. When Penelope retired, Sophia took over as the librarian. She worked tirelessly to preserve the library's collection and added new books regularly. Through Sophia's efforts, Penelope's legacy of excellence in fostering knowledge continued to thrive.

When we think about legacy, we often picture it as something that's left behind after we're gone. But what if we flipped that idea on its head? What if our legacy was something we're creating right now, in this very moment? This is what "Legacy In Forming Excellence" is all about.

A legacy isn't just a memory—it's a guiding light for others on their own journeys of discovery and growth. It's the wisdom we've gained, the values we hold dear, the love we've given, and the difference we've made. Think of it as our footprint in the sands of time, shaped by our actions, choices, and contributions.

Excellence isn't a finish line—it's a path we choose to walk every day. It's about learning, growing, and striving to be the best we can be. It's about setting high standards, refusing to settle for "good enough," and pushing beyond our comfort zones. Excellence is a mindset, a promise we make to ourselves, and a way of life.

Our legacy shapes excellence in two beautiful ways. First, it sets a standard of excellence for others to aspire to. Our actions and achievements become a benchmark, inspiring others to reach for the same heights. Second, our legacy offers valuable lessons and insights that can help others on their own journey to excellence.

"Legacy In Forming Excellence" is all about making a lasting impact through our pursuit of excellence. It's about understanding that our actions and decisions today are shaping the legacy we'll leave behind. And most importantly, it's about realizing that this legacy has the power to inspire and guide others in their own pursuit of excellence. So, let's make each day count, let's create a legacy of excellence together.

Absolutely, an individual can indeed create a legacy of excellence. It begins with a clear vision and purpose, followed by consistent actions that align with these guiding principles. The individual must strive for excellence in their chosen field, demonstrating commitment, perseverance, and resilience. They should also embody values such as integrity, respect, and responsibility, which are often associated with excellence. Over time, these efforts can culminate in a legacy that inspires and influences others. This legacy can then be passed down to future generations, serving as a benchmark of excellence and a source of inspiration. Examples of individuals who have created a legacy of excellence include leaders like Martin Luther King Jr., innovators like Steve Jobs, and humanitarians like Mother Teresa. Their legacies continue to impact the world long after their lifetimes. It's important to remember that creating a legacy of excellence is not an overnight process, but a journey that requires dedication, effort, and time.

In every moment, big or small, we're building a legacy, standing tall.
Its roots run deep, its branches with elegance, it's our Legacy in Forming Excellence.

Your legacy awaits—a canvas of whispers, a dance of constellations. Let us enjoy the journey together.

LEGACY IS ABOUT FORMING A PATH OF DISTINCTION AND
INSPIRING OTHERS TO EMBARK ON THE JOURNEY OF GREATNESS.

Chapter 2: Challenging Inner Critic

Navigating Self-Doubt and Cultivating Self-Compassion

Welcome to a journey where your inner critic becomes your trusted companion. We all have an inner voice which keeps talking to us. Sometimes it makes us conscious and sometimes it makes you under confident. Picture it as a curious friend who sometimes oversteps but ultimately wants the best for you. This inner voice—the one that whispers doubts, fears, and insecurities—is part of your story. But what if we could rewrite that story? What if we could transform this critic into an ally, cheering us on instead of holding us back?

In this chapter, we'll explore ways to silence the harsh judgments and cultivate self-compassion, we embark on a journey to challenge our inner critic. We'll explore practical strategies to quiet its noise and foster a kinder, more supportive relationship with ourselves. So, grab a cozy blanket, settle in, and let's dive into the art of embracing your inner ally.

The journey mentioned here is a metaphorical one. It's about personal growth and self-discovery. The "inner critic" refers to the negative voice inside us that often criticizes and doubts our abilities. This voice can be quite loud and persistent, causing us to feel bad about ourselves.

1. Understanding the Inner Critic

Meet The Inner Saboteur

Imagine a little gremlin hiding inside your mind. We'll call it the "Inner Saboteur." Its mission? To mess with your progress and happiness. This saboteur is sneaky. It tiptoes around, whispering negative thoughts. It's like a ninja in your brain, ready to disrupt your confidence. The saboteur loves fear. It magnifies your worries, making them seem scarier than they really are. It's like turning a tiny ant into a giant monster. These hidden aspects of our psyche undermine our progress, success, and well-being. It can manifest as self-doubt, negative self-talk, fear of failure, or self-sabotaging behaviours. Our inner critic is like a stealthy saboteur, lurking in the shadows of our mind. It feeds on our vulnerabilities, replaying past mistakes and magnifying our flaws. Sometimes, this little gremlin trips you up. It whispers, "Don't take that risk" or "What if they judge you?" But guess what? Picture a cat chasing its shadow. The saboteur thrives on negativity, just like that cat. It feeds off doubts and insecurities. If left unchecked, the saboteur becomes a barrier to growth and fulfilment. It stops you from growing, trying new things, and reaching your full potential. But what if we could pat its head and say, "Hey, let's be friends"?

Recognizing Its Whispers

Begin by tuning in to your inner dialogue. Your inner critic, though it masquerades as a voice of reason, often dances to the rhythm of fear. Pay attention to those moments when self-doubt tiptoes in—whether it's during a nerve-wracking presentation, before a promising date, or while chasing a fresh goal. Imagine it as a familiar melody, playing softly in the background. For instance, picture yourself standing at the edge of that metaphorical diving board, contemplating whether to take the plunge into a new venture. Your inner critic whispers, "What if you fail?" But remember, awareness is your compass for transformation.

2. Silencing the Inner Critic

Challenge the Evidence

When your inner critic declares, "You can't do this," ask for evidence. We all have an inner voice that tends to be critical, judgmental, and self-sabotaging. This voice is often referred to as the "inner critic." It's essential to notice when this inner critic shows up. It might be subtle, but its impact can be significant. The roots of our inner critic often trace back to our childhood. It might echo the voice of a parent, teacher, or authority figure. This negativity is evolutionary, driven by our ancient fight-or-flight mechanism. Detecting danger was crucial for survival in our early human history, but today, it can hinder our growth. Our inner critic believes it has an important role: to keep us safe, prevent risks, and avoid danger. However, it hasn't caught up with our modern, relatively safe environment.

- When your inner critic declares, "You can't do this," pause and ask for evidence:
    - Is it based on facts or assumptions?
    - More often than not, it's the latter—assumptions fuelled by fear or self-doubt.
- Challenge those assumptions:
    - Dig deeper. What evidence supports or refutes them?
    - Seek proof of your capabilities and achievements.
    - Remember your past successes—times when you defied your inner critic and achieved something remarkable.

Reframe Negative Thoughts

Replace self-critical thoughts with empowering ones. Instead of "I'm terrible at public speaking," try "I'm improving with practice." Reframing shifts the narrative from defeat to growth.

Give an attempt to befriend your inner critic. Instead of trying to eliminate the inner critic (which is challenging), aim to befriend it. Acknowledge its presence but don't let it dictate your actions. Remind yourself that you are a resourceful adult capable of growth and resilience.

Practice Self-Compassion

Imagine treating a friend who stumbles with kindness. Now apply that compassion to yourself. Acknowledge imperfections without judgment. Embrace your humanity. Self-compassion fuels resilience.

Start taking actions. Ground yourself, breathe, and allow any emotional discomfort caused by negative thoughts. Commit to moving towards what excites you, even if your inner critic protests. Prove your inner critic wrong by taking steps toward your goals.

Acknowledge it, but don't let it run the show. You've got this! Remember, we all have this little saboteur. The key is to recognize it, give it a nod, and keep moving forward!

3. Cultivating Self-Compassion

Mindful Self-Talk

Catch your inner critic mid-sentence. Replace harsh words with gentle encouragement. "It's okay to make mistakes," you might say. Treat yourself as you would a cherished friend.

Celebrate Progress

Acknowledge small victories. Celebrate efforts, not just outcomes. Each step forward is a triumph. Your inner critic may protest but remind it that growth is messy and imperfect.

Seek Support

Share your struggles with trusted friends or a therapist. Vulnerability breaks the inner critic's grip. You're not alone in this journey.

Challenging our inner critic requires patience and persistence. As we silence its negativity, we create space for self-compassion to flourish. Remember, you're not battling alone—millions face the same struggle. Embrace imperfection, celebrate progress, and be kind to yourself. The tip of life lies in nurturing your inner dialogue—one compassionate thought at a time.

<table><tr><td>

Short Examples:

One day, Maya stumbled upon a workshop on self-compassion. The instructor encouraged her to challenge Mr. Doubtful. So, she painted a canvas filled with vibrant colours, embracing her imperfections. She titled it "Courage."

At the art exhibition, a young girl stood before Maya's painting. Tears welled up in her eyes. "This speaks to my soul," she said. Maya realized that her inner critic had been wrong all along.

</td></tr></table>

From then on, whenever Mr. Doubtful spoke up, Maya would smile and say, "Thank you for your opinion, but I choose courage."

On race day, Alex felt his legs ache, and doubt crept in. But then he noticed a fellow runner struggling. She had tears in her eyes. Alex slowed down, ran alongside her, and said, "We've got this."

Captain Critical protested, but Alex ignored him. He encouraged the woman, reminding her of her strength. Together, they crossed the finish line.

As Alex caught his breath, he realized that challenging his inner critic wasn't just about himself—it was about lifting others too.

EMBRACE THE CHALLENGE OF YOUR INNER CRITIC,
FOR IT IS NOT AN ENEMY BUT A GUIDE.

Chapter 3: Mindfulness

The power of being fully present in each moment

Delve into the concept of mindfulness and present moment awareness to enjoy the power of present moment. In this chapter, let us explore the significance and practical techniques to cultivate them.

Mindfulness is a practice that involves intentionally directing our attention to the present moment without judgment. It's about being fully aware of our thoughts, feelings, bodily sensations, and the environment around us. By cultivating mindfulness, we learn to observe our experiences without getting entangled in them. This heightened awareness allows us to respond to life's challenges with clarity and compassion. Whether through meditation, mindful breathing, or simply paying attention to everyday activities, mindfulness empowers us to live more fully, reduce stress, and appreciate the richness of each passing moment.

This leads to various benefits:

- Improved Mental Well-Being with reduced Anxiety.
- Mindfulness cultivates emotional intelligence. By being present in the moment, you learn to observe your emotions without judgment. This leads to

better emotional regulation and a more balanced mood.

- Physical Health Benefits like Normal Blood Pressure, Boosted Immune System, Better Sleep and much more.
- Cognitive Enhancements like Sharper Focus and Attention, Increased Creativity, Improved Memory, Enhanced Relationships, Empathy and Compassion, Active Listening, Stress Reduction and Resilience, Stress Management, Resilience and even the Spiritual Growth.
- Research indicates that mindfulness can alter the structure and function of the brain. It slows brain aging, reduces symptoms of anxiety and depression, and contributes to an overall sense of well-being.
- Mindfulness encourages empathy, compassion, and kindness. When you relate to others and yourself with acceptance and understanding, your relationships flourish.

Remember that mindfulness is a practice—a lifelong journey. Regularity and patience yield the most significant benefits.

Present moment awareness is the exquisite art of being fully attuned to the here and now, without allowing our minds to wander into the labyrinth of past regrets or future uncertainties. Imagine savouring your favourite ice cream—a delightful swirl of creamy sweetness. Are you truly present, fully tasting and experiencing it, or is your mind already planning tomorrow's tasks or replaying yesterday's conversations? Being aware of the present moment means immersing yourself in the velvety textures, the dance of flavours on your taste buds, and the gentle coolness that kisses your palate. It's about sipping life's richness sip by sip, fully engaged in the taste of the present, as if time itself slows down to honour this fleeting sweetness.

> **The Moon Cannot Be Stolen**
>
> Ryokan, a Zen master, lived a simple life in a hut at the foot of a mountain. One evening, a thief visited the hut but found nothing to steal. Ryokan returned and caught the thief. Instead of anger, he offered his clothes as a gift. The bewildered thief took them and left.
>
> Naked, Ryokan sat watching the moon. He mused, "Poor fellow, I wish I could give him this beautiful moon."
>
> This story illustrates selflessness and the ability to find beauty even in challenging circumstances. This is the true power of mindfulness.

Few simple ways to practice mindfulness daily is as follows:

- Simple meditation: Find a quiet space and sit comfortably. Focus on your breath—notice the sensations as air flows in through your nostrils and out of your mouth. Gradually expand your awareness to include sounds, sensations, and thoughts. If your mind wanders, gently bring it back to your breath. Start with just a few minutes a day and gradually increase the duration.

- Open Awareness: Choose a routine activity (e.g., eating, walking, showering). Pay attention to the sensations in your body—both physical and emotional. Breathe deeply, allowing your abdomen to expand fully. Engage all your senses—observe what you see, hear, feel, smell, and taste. Practice "single-tasking"—fully immerse yourself in the present moment. Let thoughts and emotions come and go without judgment.

- Mindful Wakeup: Begin your day with intention. Set a positive tone by focusing on your purpose for the day. As you wake up, take a few mindful breaths. Observe the sensation of each inhale and exhale.

- Mindful Eating: Pay attention to your meal. Savor each bite, noticing flavors, textures, and smells. Put away distractions (phones, screens) and eat slowly, appreciating the nourishment. Be fully present during meals, even if they're brief.

- Mindful Walking: Take a walk outdoors. Feel the ground beneath your feet. Notice the rhythm of your steps, the air on your skin, and the sights around you. Let go of distractions and immerse yourself in the present moment.

Why is Being Present Important?

Being present is crucial for our overall well-being and mental health. It allows us to fully engage with the present moment, rather than getting lost in thoughts about the past or worries about the future. Here are some reasons why being present is essential:

- **Stress Reduction:** When we stay present, we handle life one step at a time. Challenges and tasks seem more manageable because our mind isn't racing ahead to tomorrow's worries or lingering on yesterday's problems. By focusing on the present, we reduce the mental burden of anticipating what might happen next.
- **Anxiety Reduction:** Anxiety often arises from fears about the future or regrets about the past. When we stay present, we give less power to anxious thoughts. By grounding ourselves in the "now," we become more attuned to our surroundings and less preoccupied with what might go wrong. This shift in focus can significantly reduce anxiety levels.
- **Enhanced Creativity:** A clear, focused mind is a fertile ground for creativity. When distractions fade

away, our brain has space to explore new ideas and connections. Being present allows us to tap into our intuition and inspiration. Whether it's solving a problem, writing, or creating art, being fully present enhances our ability to think creatively.

Being present is not just about mindfulness; it's about actively participating in our own lives. By staying in the moment, we can reduce stress, manage anxiety, and unlock our creative potential. So, let's practice being present and embrace the richness of each passing second.

Techniques to Enhance Mindfulness and Present Moment Awareness

In our fast-paced lives, cultivating mindfulness and staying present is essential for our mental and emotional well-being. These techniques can help you connect with the present moment, reduce stress, and enhance your overall quality of life:

- **Mindful Breathing:** Set aside a few minutes each day to focus solely on your breath:

  - How: Find a quiet space, sit comfortably, and close your eyes. Pay attention to each inhalation and exhalation. When your mind inevitably wanders (as minds tend to do), gently bring it back to the breath. Feel the rise and fall of your chest or the coolness of the air entering your nostrils. This practice anchors you in the present moment.

- **Grounding Techniques:** Ground yourself to reconnect with your immediate environment:

- How: Engage your senses. Notice the texture of objects around you—the roughness of a wooden table, the softness of a fabric, or the coolness of a stone. Listen to sounds—the distant hum of traffic, birds chirping, or the rustle of leaves. Observe colours—the vibrant green of grass, the soothing blue of the sky. Grounding brings you back to the here and now.

- **Body Scan:** Foster awareness by a body scan of physical sensations:

- How: Lie down or sit comfortably. Start at your head and progressively move down through your body. Notice any sensations—tingling, warmth, tension, or relaxation. Be curious about what you feel without judgment. This practice helps you tune in to your body's signals and promotes a sense of presence.

- **Mindful Walking:** Turn your daily walk into a mindful practice:

- How: As you walk, pay attention to each step. Feel the ground beneath your feet—the texture of pavement, grass, or sand. Notice your posture—stand tall, shoulders relaxed. Be present with the rhythm of movement—the sway of your arms, the lift of your legs. Walking mindfully transforms a mundane activity into a moment of awareness.

- **Mindful Listening:** Truly listen when conversing with others:

  - How: Put away distractions. Focus on the speaker's words, tone, and emotions. Avoid planning your response while they talk. Instead, immerse yourself in the dialogue. Notice the nuances—their pauses, the inflections in their voice, and the emotions behind their words. Listening mindfully deepens connections and enriches your interactions.

- **Mindful Eating:** Transform meals into mindful experiences:

  - How: Before you eat, take a moment to appreciate your food. Savor the flavours—the sweetness of a ripe mango, the warmth of soup, the crunch of fresh vegetables. Pay attention to textures—the creaminess of yogurt, the juiciness of a grape. Chew slowly and deliberately. Avoid distractions like screens or multitasking. Eating mindfully nourishes both body and soul.

- **Meditation:** Regular meditation sessions train your mind to stay present:

- How: Find a comfortable spot, sit or lie down, and close your eyes. Choose a meditation technique—mindfulness meditation, loving-kindness meditation, or any other that resonates with you. Focus on your breath, a mantra, or a visual image. When thoughts arise (and they will), gently guide your attention back to your chosen focus. Over time, meditation enhances your present moment awareness.

Remember, being present isn't about perfection; it's about practice. Experiment with these techniques, adapt them to your lifestyle, and discover what works best for you. As you cultivate mindfulness, you'll find that life becomes richer, more vibrant, and deeply fulfilling.

Remember, practicing mindfulness is a journey. Start small, be patient with yourself, and gradually integrate these techniques into your daily life. The rewards—greater peace, reduced stress, and heightened awareness—are well worth the effort.

A Useless Life: A farmer grew old and could no longer work the fields. He spent his days sitting on the porch, seemingly idle. His son, still tending to the farm, grew frustrated. "He's of no use anymore," the son thought.

In his frustration, the son built a wooden coffin, placed his father inside, and dragged it to the edge of a high cliff. Just before pushing it over, he heard a tapping from inside. The father calmly said, "I know you're going to throw me over, but before you do, may I suggest something? Save this good wood coffin. Your children might need it someday."

The story reminds us that even seemingly idle moments have purpose, and impermanence teaches us to appreciate what we have.

Acceptance and Letting Go: Embracing the Present Moment

Imagine standing on the shore of a tranquil lake, the water reflecting the hues of the setting sun. You notice a leaf floating on the surface, carried by gentle ripples. As you watch, you realize that the leaf doesn't fight against the current; it doesn't resist its journey. Instead, it surrenders to the flow, allowing itself to be carried wherever the water takes it.

Mindfulness encourages us to be like that leaf—to accept what is, even if it's uncomfortable. Letting go of resistance and allowing experiences to unfold naturally is a powerful practice that can transform our lives.

The Art of Acceptance

The Art of Acceptance is a profound skill that holds immense significance in our lives. It involves the ability to fully embrace the entire spectrum of our thoughts and emotions, all while remaining committed to what truly matters. Imagine it as a mental workout: just as we stretch our muscles during exercise, we deliberately practice acceptance during moments when it seemingly doesn't matter. These small emotional stretches build our overall acceptance skills, ensuring that we're equipped to handle life's challenges when they do matter. Acceptance isn't about avoiding discomfort or clinging to fleeting emotions; rather, it's about navigating life's bittersweet moments with grace and resilience. Whether it's accepting the passing of time, the changing dynamics of relationships, or the inevitable ups and downs, this art allows us to find peace amidst life's complexities.

> **The Broken Mug:** Sarah loved her grandmother's antique China mug. It was delicate, adorned with delicate roses, and held memories of cozy afternoons spent sipping tea. One day, as she washed it, it slipped from her hands and shattered into pieces. Sarah felt a surge of panic and sadness. But then she remembered mindfulness.
>
> Instead of berating herself or mourning the loss, she sat with the broken pieces. She noticed the jagged edges, the faded colours, and the history etched into each shard. She accepted that accidents happen, and sometimes cherished things break. She let go of the

need to fix it or replace it. And in that acceptance, she found peace.

The Unfinished Story: Alex was a writer. He had started a novel—a grand adventure set in a mythical land—but life got busy, and the manuscript gathered dust. Every time he looked at it, guilt gnawed at him. He felt like a failure for not finishing what he started.

One day, during a mindfulness meditation, he realized that the story wasn't incomplete; it was merely paused. He accepted that creativity ebbs and flows, and sometimes stories need time to breathe. Alex let go of the pressure to finish and allowed himself to enjoy the process. Eventually, the words flowed again, and the novel found its ending.

The Liberation of Letting Go

Have you ever found yourself caught in the web of indecision? You know that place where you're juggling options, analysing every angle, and wondering if you should take that leap or stay put? It's like standing at a crossroads with a thousand paths stretching out before you. Each one whispers, "Choose me!" And you're left feeling stuck, ankle-deep in the mud of uncertainty.

But guess what? Clarity sometimes tiptoes in when you least expect it. It's like a tiny sunbeam breaking through the clouds. And it says, "Hey, friend, maybe it's time to let go." Not because you're giving up, but because you're making space. You're shedding the weight of what doesn't quite fit your journey. And in that release, there's freedom—a lightness that opens doors.

So, you take a deep breath, loosen your grip, and watch as that burden floats away. Suddenly, the fog lifts, and you see the path ahead. It's clearer now. And what happens next? Well, that's the magic part—you'll know when it arrives. Maybe it's a new adventure, a fresh perspective, or simply a sense of peace. But one thing's for sure: letting go can be the sweetest liberation of all.

The Balloon Release: At a mindfulness retreat, participants were given helium balloons. Each balloon represented a worry, fear, or regret. As they released them into the sky, they whispered their burdens to the wind. The balloons floated away, and with them went the weight of their troubles.

One woman hesitated. Her balloon was labelled "past mistakes." She clung to it, afraid to let go. But then she realized that holding on didn't change the past—it only weighed her down. With tears in her eyes, she released the balloon, feeling a sense of liberation she hadn't known before.

The Autumn Tree: In a quiet park, there stood an ancient oak tree. Its leaves turned golden in the fall, and as winter approached, they fell one by one. The tree didn't fight it;

it didn't cling to its foliage. It accepted the changing seasons with grace.

Under that tree, a woman sat, contemplating her own life. She had lost loved ones, faced heartaches, and weathered storms. But like the tree, she realized that letting go was essential. She accepted the impermanence of all things—the leaves, the seasons, and even her own emotions. And in that acceptance, she found resilience.

Mindfulness invites us to be present—to observe life without judgment, to accept what is, and to let go of what no longer serves us. Like the leaf on the lake, we can surrender to the currents of existence, trusting that they will carry us where we need to go. So, my friend, embrace acceptance, and let go. The journey awaits.

Practice Non-Judgmental Observation

Imagine you're just sitting back, watching the world go by, taking everything in stride. That's what non-judgmental observation is all about! It's like being at a movie, enjoying the show without worrying if it's good or bad. You're in the moment, soaking it all up, no labels, no biases. It's pretty cool, right? You get to understand others better, and it's like opening a door to new perspectives. Plus, it makes conversations so much more interesting! So, why not give it a try? It's a great way to grow and make our interactions with others more meaningful

Picture this: You're sitting in a bustling café, sipping your favourite latte. The aroma of freshly baked pastries fills the air, and the hum of conversation surrounds you. It's a moment of quiet reflection—a chance to observe without judgment.

Across the room, a young couple huddles over their laptops. Their faces are etched with determination, fingers flying across the keyboard. They're in their own world, chasing dreams, and you wonder what stories they hold—their hopes, their fears, their late-night epiphanies.

At the next table, an elderly woman sits alone. Her weathered hands cradle a worn-out journal. She writes with deliberate strokes, pen gliding across the pages. Perhaps she's chronicling a lifetime of memories—the laughter, the tears, the missed chances. Or maybe she's creating something entirely new—a poem, a letter, a recipe passed down through generations.

Outside the window, raindrops tap a rhythm on the glass. A street musician plays a soulful tune on his guitar, eyes closed, lost in the melody. His music weaves through the crowd, touching hearts, bridging gaps. And you realize that every passerby has a story—a hidden chapter waiting to unfold.

Non-judgmental observation is about being fully present in these moments. It's about noticing without labelling. You see the tired eyes of the waitress, the toddler's chubby fingers reaching for a cookie, the graffiti on the brick wall. Each detail holds a universe of experiences.

And here's the magic: When you let go of judgment, you open yourself to empathy. You become a witness, not a critic. The noisy neighbour becomes a person with dreams and fears. The impatient driver becomes someone rushing to a hospital. The world transforms from black and white to a kaleidoscope of colours.

So, you take a deep breath, loosen your grip, and watch as that burden floats away. Suddenly, the fog lifts, and you see the path ahead. It's clearer now. And what happens next? Well, that's the magic part—you'll know when it arrives. Maybe it's a new adventure, a fresh perspective, or simply a sense of peace. But one thing's for sure: letting go can be the sweetest liberation of all.

Practicing non-judgmental observation can be a game-changer. It's like putting on a pair of compassionate glasses that allow you to see the world without preconceived notions. Here are some practical ways to weave this magic into your daily life:

- **Notice Your Judgments:** Start by becoming aware of those sneaky judgments that pop up like uninvited guests. When you catch yourself thinking, "Oh, that person is so X," pause. Acknowledge the judgment without judgment (meta, I know!). Awareness is the first step.
- **Label Your Judgments:** Give your judgments a name. Imagine them as little thought bubbles floating by. Instead of saying, "That guy is lazy," try, "Ah, there's my 'lazy' judgment again." Labelling helps create distance and reduces their power over you.
- **People-Watching:** Next time you're at a café or a park, people-watch. Not in a creepy way, of course! Observe without attaching labels. Notice their expressions, body language, and interactions. Imagine their stories—the joys, struggles, and quirks.
- **Observe Nature:** Spend time in nature. Watch the leaves rustle, birds' flit about, and ants' scurry. Nature doesn't judge; it just exists. Learn from it. Maybe even hug a tree (no judgment here!).
- **Mindful Self-Talk:** Pay attention to your inner chatter. When you spill coffee, do you immediately think, "I'm so clumsy!"? Replace it with, "Oops, a little coffee mishap." Be kind to yourself; you're a work in progress.
- **Affirmations:** Choose affirmations that promote non-judgmental thinking. Repeat them like mantras. For example:
  - "I release judgment and embrace understanding."
  - "Every person has a unique journey."
  - "I see beyond appearances."

- **Step Outside Your Comfort Zone:** Engage with people or situations you'd usually avoid. Maybe strike up a conversation with that person in the corner at the party. Who knows? They might surprise you.
- **Observe Your Thoughts:** Imagine your mind as a curious scientist. Observe your thoughts without getting entangled. When you think, "She's rude," ask, "Is that a fact or my perception?"
- **Assess Results Without Judgment:** After practicing non-judgment, reflect. How did it feel? Did you notice any shifts in your interactions? Remember, its progress, not perfection.

And here's the secret: Non-judgmental observation isn't about being passive. It's about seeing clearly, understanding deeply, and connecting authentically. So, go forth, my friend, and observe—with kindness and curiosity.

MINDFULNESS IS THE KEY TO UNLOCKING THE FULL POTENTIAL OF
YOUR MIND. IT'S ABOUT SAVORING THE RICHNESS OF THE MOMENT.

Chapter 4: Life Milestones and Turning Points

Reflect on significant moments that shapes life!

Life, my dear friend, is a grand tapestry—a weaving of moments, emotions, and milestones. Imagine an ancient loom, its wooden frame stretching across time and space. Each thread, delicate yet resilient, represents an experience—a laughter-filled afternoon, a tear-streaked night, a sunrise that whispered secrets to the mountains.

Let me spin you a tale of this intricate fabric:

Threads of Experiences: Picture a young artist, her fingers stained with paint. She dips her brush into the palette of life, creating vibrant strokes on her canvas. The first kiss—the taste of summer strawberries and stolen glances—is a crimson thread. The thrill of conquering fears—a rollercoaster ride, heart pounding—is a golden thread. And the quiet solitude of a moonlit beach—a silver thread that shimmers with memories.

Hues of Relationships: Our tapestry is awash with colours. There's the azure blue of friendship—the kind that laughs with you until tears blur the lines. The deep green of family—the roots that anchor us, even when storms rage.

And the fiery red of love—passionate, consuming, leaving imprints like footprints in wet sand.

Moments That Mould Us: In a bustling café, a stranger shares their story. Their words, like a potter's hands, shape our clay hearts. We learn empathy, compassion—the art of understanding. And in the quiet of a hospital room, a nurse cradles a newborn. Her touch, gentle as a breeze, leaves an indelible mark. The baby's first cry—a symphony of hope—echoes through generations.

Fingerprints on Our Hearts: Think of the people who waltz into our lives. The elderly neighbour who bakes cookies and dispenses wisdom. The childhood friend who knows our secrets—the ones we buried beneath treehouse floors. Their fingerprints linger, etching love letters on the walls of our souls.

Circumstances That Test Our Mettle: Life isn't all sunsets and soft breezes. Sometimes, it's a tempest—a wild sea that tosses us about. Picture a mountaineer scaling Everest. The biting cold, the thin air—it tests their resolve. But with each step, they become more than flesh and bone. They become resilience, courage—the very fabric of survival.

And so, my friend, what shapes our lives? It's not just the grand moments—the graduations, weddings, or promotions. It's the ordinary seconds—the laughter over burnt toast, the tears shed in solitude. It's the threads we weave, the colours we choose, and the stories we tell.

So, let's raise our imaginary goblets (filled with metaphorical grape juice, of course) and toast to this magnificent tapestry. May it be rich, vibrant, and woven with love.

1. Graduations: Crossing Thresholds

Graduation—a word that resonates with achievement, growth, and transition. Whether it's high school, college, or postgraduate studies, graduations mark the end of one chapter and the beginning of another. The cap and gown symbolize not just academic accomplishment but also resilience, late-night study sessions, and friendships forged over shared stress.

Remember the exhilaration of tossing your graduation cap into the air? That split second encapsulates years of hard work, sleepless nights, and dreams realized. As you walked across the stage, you carried not just a diploma but also memories of late-night pizza run, passionate debates, and the thrill of discovery.

2. Relocations: The Art of Adaptation

Moving to a new place is like opening a fresh chapter in the book of life. Whether it's across town or across continents, relocations force us to adapt, explore, and redefine our comfort zones. The unfamiliar streets become our canvas, and we paint our stories with each step.

Remember the first night in your new home? The echo of silence, the scent of unfamiliar spices wafting from neighbouring kitchens, and the thrill of discovering hidden gems—a cozy café, a park with blooming cherry blossoms, or a friendly neighbour who becomes family.

3. The Symphony of Relationships: Love, Heartbreak, and Growth

People are the heartbeats of our existence. Friends, family, mentors, and lovers—they compose the symphony of our lives. A childhood friend's loyalty, a sibling's teasing, a grandparent's wisdom—they resonate within us. Love, loss, forgiveness, and camaraderie—they mould our emotional landscape. We learn that vulnerability is strength, and connection is oxygen.

Ah, relationships—the heartbeat of our existence. Falling in love is like stepping into a sun-drenched garden. The colours are brighter, the laughter more melodic, and time dances to its own rhythm. But love isn't just about sunshine; it's also about storms. Heartbreaks teach us resilience, empathy, and the art of healing.

Remember your first crush? The butterflies in your stomach, the stolen glances, and the thrill of a shared secret. And then, the ache—the realization that love isn't always forever. But from those fragments, we rebuild, learning to love ourselves and others more authentically.

4. Personal Achievements: Triumphs and Lessons

Our personal achievements—small or grand—define us. It could be facing a difficult exam, completing a marathon, or publishing your first poem. These moments are like stepping stones across a rushing river. They propel us forward, reminding us of our capabilities.

Remember the day you held your published book in your hands? The weight of the pages, the smell of ink, and the knowledge that your words would touch hearts. Or perhaps it was the day you conquered your fear of public speaking, standing tall before an audience, heart racing but voice unwavering.

5. Moments of Self-Discovery: The Quiet Revolution

Amid life's noise, there are whispers of self-discovery. These moments don't come with fanfare; they tiptoe into our consciousness. It's the realization that you're more resilient than you thought, the acceptance of imperfections, and the quiet revolution of understanding your purpose.

Remember the night you sat alone under a star-studded sky? The questions that surfaced—the "why" and "who am I?" The answers didn't arrive in a lightning bolt; they seeped into your bones, shaping your choices, relationships, and passions.

Nicolae's Mindfulness Journey: Nicolae, a corporate executive, found himself perpetually stressed and disconnected from his inner self. Amid the chaos of board meetings and deadlines, he stumbled upon mindfulness. It began with a simple practice: sitting quietly for a few minutes each day, observing his breath. Gradually, he noticed subtle shifts—a calmer mind, heightened awareness, and a newfound clarity. Nicolae's tale is one of resilience, introspection, and a relentless pursuit of enlightenment. His journey unfolded like a quiet revolution, inviting him to embrace mindfulness fully and explore the depths of his consciousness.

The Daily Reflection Ritual: Emma, a young artist, struggled with creative blocks and self-doubt. She decided to embark on a daily ritual: sitting by her window each morning, sipping tea, and reflecting. In those quiet moments, she observed the play of light on leaves, listened to distant birdsong, and allowed her mind to wander. Gradually, her mental clutter dissolved, making space for inspiration. Emma's quiet revolution was not loud or dramatic—it was the gentle turning of a key that unlocked her creativity and inner wisdom.

The Language of Silence: Rajiv, a linguistics professor, spent years studying languages spoken by people across the globe. Yet, he felt a void within—an untranslatable emotion that eluded words. One day, during a silent meditation retreat, he experienced a profound shift. In the stillness, he realized that silence itself was a language—one that spoke directly to the soul. Rajiv's quiet revolution involved unlearning the need for constant chatter and embracing the eloquence of silence.

The Unplugged Adventure: Sarah, a tech-savvy entrepreneur, decided to disconnect from screens and notifications for a week. She retreated to a remote cabin, surrounded by towering pines and a serene lake. Without distractions, she listened to her heartbeat, watched sunsets, and journaled her thoughts. In that unplugged solitude, Sarah discovered her true desires, fears, and dreams. Her quiet revolution was a deliberate step away from the noise, leading her toward authenticity and purpose.

The Whispering Forest: Mark, a city dweller, joined a hiking group for a weekend expedition. As he trekked through ancient forests, he noticed how the trees communicated—a network of roots and whispers. Mark's own thoughts echoed in response. In those woods, he realized that self-discovery wasn't about shouting his identity; it was about listening—to nature, to his intuition, and to the quiet revolution unfolding within. Mark returned home with a heart full of forest secrets and a newfound reverence for stillness.

6. The Crossroads of Choices

Life unfolds at crossroads. Each decision—a fork in the road—shapes our trajectory. The choice of college, career, or partner—the ripple effect is profound. Sometimes, we stumble; other times, we soar. The path less taken may lead to unexpected vistas. Our choices define us, revealing courage or caution, audacity or prudence.

7. The Echoes of Adversity

Adversity—the chisel that sculpts resilience. Life isn't a smooth sail, storms brew, waves crash. Illness, heartbreak, failure—they visit uninvited. Yet, within these tempests lie hidden gifts. We discover our inner fortitude, the art of surrender, and the beauty of scars. Adversity shapes our empathy; it teaches us to hold space for others' pain.

8. The Canvas of Creativity

In the grand symphony of life, creativity stands as the most enchanting note. It swirls through our days, weaving magic into the mundane. Whether we wield a paintbrush, write code, or bake bread, creativity infuses every moment with purpose. It's the poet's verses that echo across centuries, the architect's blueprints that shape skylines, and the gardener's blooms that whisper secrets to the wind.

Creativity is the silent muse, urging us to embrace our inner artist. It tiptoes into our consciousness, whispering, "You are a creator; your life is your canvas." And so, we pick up our brushes, our pens, our spatulas, and we begin. With each stroke, each line of code, each kneading of dough, we breathe life into our visions. The blank canvas becomes a universe waiting to be painted, a story yearning to be told.

Imagination is our dance partner, twirling us through realms uncharted. We pirouette on the edge of reality, daring to dream in vivid hues. The poet spins sonnets from stardust, the musician orchestrates symphonies from heartbeats, and the chef concocts flavors that ignite memories. Creativity invites us to waltz with the impossible, to tango with the intangible. In its rhythm, we find solace, purpose, and sheer delight.

Creativity is rebellion against monotony, a rebellion that dares us to break free from the ordinary. It whispers, "Why settle for grey when you can have a kaleidoscope?" So, we splash colours onto our canvases, string words into constellations, and plant seeds that bloom into gardens of wonder. It's in the swirl of a dancer's skirt, the brushstroke of a graffiti artist, and the algorithm that unravels the mysteries of the universe.

Our dreams are the palette, and creativity is the brush that paints them into existence. We sketch castles in the air, build bridges between galaxies, and compose symphonies that resonate across time. Creativity is the alchemy that turns raw materials into masterpieces, chaos into cosmos. It's the spark that ignites revolutions, the lullaby that cradles our souls.

So let us heed the whispers of creativity. Let us dance, paint, write, and bake. Let us honour the artist within, for our lives are vast canvases waiting to be adorned. In every stroke, we find purpose; in every creation, we discover our essence. Creativity colours our existence, making it a masterpiece worth celebrating.

9. The Fragility of Time

Time, like a silent river, flows through our lives, its currents shaping our existence in ways both profound and imperceptible. We often squander it, unaware of its true value—the elusive currency we spend without realizing its worth. Each tick of the clock accumulates into days, months, and years, etching lines on our faces and memories in our hearts.

Birthdays come and go, like milestones marking our journey. They remind us of the inexorable passage of time, urging us to reflect on the chapters written and the ones yet to unfold. With each passing year, we accumulate experiences—some joyous, others bittersweet—but all contributing to the mosaic of our lives.

Seasons change, painting the canvas of existence with vibrant hues. Spring whispers promises of renewal, summer blazes with intensity, autumn sheds its golden tears, and winter wraps us in contemplative stillness. Time dances through these seasons, weaving stories of growth, loss, and resilience.

And then there are the wrinkles, etched by laughter and tears alike. They map the laughter lines around our eyes, the furrows of worry on our brows. These creases tell tales of resilience, of battles fought and joys celebrated. They are the imprints of a life well-lived—a testament to the passage of time.

In this relentless flow, we learn to cherish moments. The fiery sunsets that paint the sky in hues of orange and pink— their fleeting beauty reminds us to pause, to breathe, and to marvel. The shared meals—the clinking of cutlery, the warmth of companionship—they become our sustenance, nourishing not just our bodies but our souls.

Time shapes our priorities. It nudges us to mend broken bonds, to reach out across chasms of hurt and misunderstanding. It whispers, "Forgive, for life is too short to harbour grudges." It encourages us to chase our passions—to write that novel, climb that mountain, or strum that forgotten guitar. It beckons us to savour the ordinary—the morning coffee, the rustle of leaves, the touch of a loved one's hand.

And so, we navigate this river of time, sometimes drifting, sometimes swimming against the current. We learn that its value lies not in accumulation but in how we spend it—in the love we give, the dreams we pursue, and the memories we create. For in the grand tapestry of existence, time is the thread that binds us all—a fragile, precious thread that weaves our stories into eternity.

10. The Legacy We Leave

In the grand tapestry of existence, our legacy transcends mere material wealth or lofty titles. Instead, it finds its abode in the hearts we touch—the ripples of kindness, compassion, and authenticity that extend far beyond our mortal years. Whether we nurture saplings into towering trees, pen words that ignite minds, or raise resilient children who carry our essence forward, our impact reverberates through the annals of time. We are not solitary stars; rather, we join a cosmic constellation—a collective of souls weaving the fabric of the universe itself. Our legacy, intangible yet profound, etches its mark upon eternity.

Our Mosaic of Moments

Imagine a sun-kissed afternoon. You, with your heart as open as a blooming flower, sit on a park bench. The breeze carries whispers—the laughter of children, the secrets shared by old friends. These moments, like shards of stained glass, fit together to create a mosaic. Each piece, unique and irreplaceable, adds depth to our life's stained-glass window.

Graduations: Picture a cap tossed into the air, sunlight catching its flight. A graduate stands at the edge of possibility. Their diploma—a parchment of dreams—holds stories of late-night study sessions, friendships forged over caffeine, and that one epic PowerPoint presentation. Graduations are not just about mortarboards; they're about the courage to leap into the unknown.

Relocations: Ah, the bittersweet dance of packing boxes! A map unfolds, tracing routes across continents. The smell of cardboard mingles with nostalgia. You leave behind familiar streets, but your heart becomes a nomad. In a new city, you discover hidden cafés, quirky bookshops, and neighbours who share recipes for cosmic cookies. Relocations are like bookmarks in the novel of life.

Relationships: Love, my friend, is a palette of hues. There's the blush pink of a first crush—the way your heart flutters like a startled butterfly. Then comes the cobalt blue of companionship—the kind that laughs at your terrible jokes and forgives your mismatched socks. And let's not forget the fiery orange of passion—the kind that ignites bonfires and writes poetry on skin.

Personal Triumphs: Imagine a marathon runner, sweat-slicked and determined. Their finish line isn't just marked by a ribbon; it's etched with memories. The first step—a whisper of courage. The halfway point—a battle against doubt. And the final sprint—a roar of victory. Personal triumphs are medals we wear on our souls.

Whispers of Self-Discovery: Close your eyes. Listen. The universe murmurs secrets. In a quiet room, you confront your fears—the shadows that lurk under your bed. You read books that unravel galaxies within you. Self-discovery is a cosmic voyage—a telescope pointed inward. It reveals constellations of resilience, vulnerability, and the stardust of authenticity.

Guiding Stars: Look up. The night sky is a celestial roadmap. Orion winks, and Cassiopeia pirouettes. Life's constellations—made of dreams, setbacks, and moonlit epiphanies—guide us. They say, "Follow your North Star."

But sometimes, it's the shooting stars—the unexpected wishes—that lead us to hidden treasure.

Embracing the Tapestry: Our lives aren't pristine canvases; they're tapestries with frayed edges. Imagine a weaver—call them Destiny—working tirelessly. They knot threads of joy, sorrow, and resilience. The vibrant threads? Those are the people we love—the ones who lend us their colors when ours fade. And the unfinished patterns? They're our dreams, still taking shape.

So, my fellow dreamer, let's raise our metaphorical goblets once more. To life—the masterpiece in progress. May we embrace the brushstrokes, the smudges, and the occasional cosmic hiccup. For perfection? It's overrated. Growth, connection, and the art of becoming—that's our true masterpiece.

Remember, we are both the sculptor and the sculpture of our life. And as we continue our journey, let's remember that the best chapters are yet to be written.

EVERY MILESTONE IS A MINIATURE VICTORY ON
THE ROAD TO ACHIEVING YOUR GOALS.

Chapter 5: Overcoming Adversity and Resilience

Resilience, bouncing back from setbacks, and finding strength

Life is a journey marked by both summits and deep valleys. Along this winding path, we inevitably encounter adversity—those unforeseen trials that push us to our limits. Whether it's a personal setback, a professional obstacle, or a health crisis, adversity is woven into the fabric of our existence. It tests our mettle, challenges our resilience, and forces us to confront our innermost fears. In the face of adversity, we have choices. We can crumble under its weight, succumbing to despair and defeat. Or we can rise like phoenixes, drawing strength from our scars and transforming adversity into opportunity. Our response to life's challenges defines our character and shapes our trajectory.

Resilience becomes our armour—a shield against the storms that threaten to engulf us. We learn to adapt, to bend without breaking. Adversity teaches us that failure is not fatal; it's merely a stepping stone toward growth. Each setback becomes a chance to rewrite our narrative, to forge a new path forward. Consider the mountaineer scaling Everest. The summit is the ultimate goal, but the journey is fraught with peril. The thin air, biting cold, and treacherous terrain test physical limits. Yet, it's in those moments of struggle that character emerges. The climber's determination, unwavering focus, and sheer willpower propel them upward. They become more than conquerors; they become legends.

Similarly, life's valleys—those dark, desolate stretches—reveal our true essence. When faced with loss, heartache, or disappointment, we discover depths of courage we never knew existed. We find solace in the embrace of loved ones, draw inspiration from stories of resilience, and learn that vulnerability is not weakness—it's the birthplace of strength. Adversity shapes our path, but it need not define us. We can emerge scarred yet undaunted, our hearts etched with the wisdom of survival. Our journey becomes a tapestry of triumphs and tribulations, each thread contributing to the masterpiece of our lives.

Embracing Adversity: The Climb of a Lifetime: In the heart of the Himalayas, where the sky kisses the earth, stands Mount Everest, a colossal sentinel that beckons adventurers from every corner of the globe. Its snow-capped peak pierces the heavens, a silent challenge to those who dare to ascend. But beyond the icy facade lies a profound metaphor—a testament to the human spirit and our unwavering quest for greatness.

Picture this: A solitary climber, bundled in layers of down, stands at Everest Base Camp. The air is thin, and the wind whispers secrets of ancient glaciers. Her breath mingles with the frost, and her heartbeat echoes in the silence. She gazes upward, tracing the jagged ridges that lead to the summit—the ultimate zenith. It's a journey marked not only by altitude but by resilience, courage, and the indomitable will to conquer the impossible.

The Summit Beckons: Our climber's name is Maya. She's not a seasoned mountaineer; she's an ordinary woman with extraordinary dreams. Her life, like all of ours, has been a mosaic of highs and lows. Yet, when adversity knocked on her door, she didn't retreat; she laced up her boots and set her sights on Everest.

As she ascends, the air grows thinner, and her lungs labour for each breath. The biting cold gnaws at her fingertips, but she presses on. The path is treacherous— a tightrope between life and oblivion. She's not alone; fellow climbers share stories around campfires. They speak of lost friends, of avalanches that swallowed entire teams, and of the mountain's fickle moods. But they also share laughter, camaraderie, and the fire of determination.

The Storm Within: One night, as the wind howls, Maya huddles in her tent. The storm rages outside, but another tempest brews within her. Doubt creeps in—an insidious whisper that questions her purpose. Why endure this suffering? Why risk frostbite, exhaustion, and the abyss? She thinks of her family, her daughter's smile, and the unfinished novel waiting back home. The summit seems distant, almost mythical.

But then she remembers the stories—the legends etched into Everest's icy walls. Sir Edmund Hillary and Tenzing Norgay, the first conquerors, who danced atop the world. Reinhold Messner, who climbed without supplemental oxygen, defying nature's rules. Their footsteps echo in her soul. They weren't immune to fear; they simply chose to dance with it.

The Triumph of Character: Maya emerges from her tent, her breath crystallizing in the frigid air. The summit looms, tantalizingly close yet impossibly far. She pushes forward, step by agonizing step. Her legs ache, her fingers numb, but her spirit soars. The thin air whispers secrets—the wisdom of ages. She thinks of resilience, of bending without breaking. Each setback becomes a rung on her ladder to the sky.

And then, as dawn blushes the peaks, she stands atop the world. The Himalayas bow to her, and the sun salutes her courage. Maya isn't just a climber; she's a legend—a testament to human tenacity. She gazes at the horizon, where valleys and summits intertwine. Life, she realizes, is Everest—a journey of resilience, of choosing to hope over despair.

Understanding Adversity

Adversity comes in various forms, and each one presents unique obstacles to overcome. Adversity refers to a state or instance of serious or continued difficulty or misfortune. It is a condition marked by challenges, setbacks, or unfavourable circumstances that test an individual's resilience and character. When faced with adversity, people often reveal their true strength and courage. Whether it's overcoming personal struggles, navigating life's hardships, or persevering through unexpected obstacles, the ability to face adversity with determination and grace defines our human spirit. In the depths of adversity, we find opportunities for growth, learning, and transformation. Let's explore some common types of adversity:

Emotional Adversity: This includes dealing with grief, heartbreak, or emotional trauma. It can leave us feeling overwhelmed and vulnerable.

Mental Adversity: Mental health challenges, such as anxiety and depression, fall into this category. Prolonged stress can take a toll on our well-being.

Physical Adversity: Health complications, injuries, or chronic illnesses create physical adversity. These conditions disrupt our daily lives and demand resilience.

Adversity isn't just an external force—it affects our mental and emotional well-being. Here's how:

Anxiety and Depression: Studies link childhood adversity to mental health conditions like anxiety and depression. The stress hormones released during tough times can leave us feeling hopeless and helpless.

Disruption of Stability: Adversity shakes our sense of stability and security. We grapple with feelings of uncertainty and fear.

Resilience is our ability to bounce back from adversity, learn, and grow stronger. Here's how to cultivate resilience:

Reframe Negative Thoughts: Instead of seeing adversity as insurmountable, look for small ways to tackle the problem. Reframe your thoughts positively.

Seek Support: Reach out to friends, family, or professionals. Social support is crucial during tough times.

Focus on What You Can Control: Some things are beyond our control. Concentrate on what you can influence and take action.

Manage Stress: Practice stress-reducing techniques like mindfulness, exercise, and adequate sleep.

Few simple strategies for overcoming adversity:

- **Resilience Identity:** Believe in your ability to bounce back.
- **Recognize the Ordinary:** Find joy in everyday moments.
- **Reframe Hardship:** View challenges as opportunities for growth.
- **Activate Social Support:** Lean on loved ones.

- **Practice Gratitude:** Appreciate what you have.
- **Reframe Problems:** Change your perspective.
- **Positive Self-Talk:** Encourage yourself.
- **Embrace Vulnerability:** It's okay to seek help.
- **Kindness to Self and Others:** Be compassionate.
- **Therapy Sessions:** Seek professional guidance.
- **Self-Care:** Prioritize physical and mental well-being.

Adversity is not our enemy; it's our teacher. It teaches us resilience, empathy, and the art of rising above challenges. So, when life throws curveballs, remember that you have the strength within you to overcome and emerge even stronger. Adversity is an inevitable part of life, presenting unexpected challenges that test our strength and resilience. Whether it's emotional turmoil, mental health struggles, or physical setbacks, how we respond matters. Resilience—the ability to bounce back, learn, and grow stronger—becomes our ally. By reframing negative thoughts, seeking support, and focusing on what we can control, we build resilience. Remember, adversity isn't our enemy; it's our teacher, shaping our character and guiding us toward growth.

Resilience isn't about avoiding adversity; it's about navigating it with courage, adaptability, and an unyielding spirit.

Resilience is the ability to cope with and recover from setbacks. It's like having an emotional spring that helps you bounce back when life throws challenges your way. Here are some strategies to build resilience:

Find a Sense of Purpose: Having a clear purpose gives meaning to life's difficulties. Whether it's building a support system, contributing to a social movement, creating art, or serving your community, having a purpose motivates you to keep going even during tough times.

Believe in Your Abilities: Confidence in your own coping abilities is crucial. Replace negative self-talk with positive affirmations. Remind yourself of your strengths and past accomplishments. Your self-esteem plays a significant role in resilience.

Develop a Strong Social Network: Surround yourself with caring, supportive people. Talking about your feelings with friends or loved ones won't magically solve your problems, but it provides emotional support, positive feedback, and potential solutions.

Embrace Change: Flexibility is key. Resilient individuals adapt to life's twists and turns. Use challenging events as opportunities for growth and exploration.

Be Optimistic: Maintain a positive outlook. Even in difficult situations, focus on what you can learn and how you can grow. Optimism helps you face adversity with greater strength.

Nurture Yourself: Self-care matters. Prioritize physical health, emotional well-being, and relaxation. Take breaks, practice mindfulness, and engage in activities that recharge you.

Develop Problem-Solving Skills: When problems arise, approach them rationally. Seek solutions rather than dwelling on the issue. Problem-solving skills enhance resilience.

> **Dream of Olympics to Para Olympics:** Peter, a talented swimmer, dreamed of winning an Olympic medal for his country. Tragically, he lost both his hands in a car accident that also claimed his father's life. Devastated, Peter discovered an old poster crafted by his father, expressing pride in his son's swimming abilities. Encouraged by his mother, Peter set a new goal: to excel in the Paralympics. Despite immense challenges, he trained relentlessly, breaking records and winning gold and silver medals for his country. Peter's resilience transformed tragedy into triumph, proving that determination knows no bounds.
>
> **The Farmer and the Donkey:** A farmer's donkey fell into a well, and the animal cried for hours. The farmer initially considered leaving it there, but he invited neighbours to help. Together, they decided to fill the well with dirt, believing the donkey was old and its life not worth saving. As they shovelled dirt, the donkey shook it off and stepped up. Eventually, the well filled, and the donkey climbed out. This story teaches us that adversity can be an opportunity for resilience and transformation.

Real-Life Stories of Heartbreak and Resilience: In our daily lives, we encounter countless stories of resilience. These are often brief but powerful accounts of human strength. One such story might be a single parent working multiple jobs to provide for their children, refusing to give up despite exhaustion. Another could be a cancer survivor who faces treatment with unwavering courage. These small, real-life moments remind us that resilience resides within us all, waiting to be summoned when needed most.

Life often throws unexpected challenges our way—times when we feel overwhelmed, exhausted, and uncertain. Yet, within these moments lies the opportunity to discover our inner strength. Here are some ways to find resilience during adversity:

Self-Reflection: Take a step back and reflect on your past experiences. Remember the times when you overcame obstacles, even when it seemed impossible. Recognize your own resilience.

Seek Support: Reach out to friends, family, or a counsellor. Sharing your feelings lightens the burden and reminds you that you're not alone.

Mindfulness and Acceptance: Practice being present in the moment. Accept the situation without judgment. Acknowledge your emotions, but don't let them consume you.

Small Steps: Break down the challenge into smaller, manageable steps. Focus on one thing at a time. Each small victory adds up to greater strength.

Positive Affirmations: Remind yourself of your capabilities. Repeat affirmations like, "I am strong," "I can handle this," and "This too shall pass."

Remember, strength isn't about being invincible; it's about persevering despite adversity. You are more resilient than you realize.

In the Bull Mother Farm on the outskirts of Madhya Pradesh's capital Bhopal, a remarkable tale of unity in adversity unfolded. Recently, a tiger intruded into the farm, stealthily entering through an 8-foot-high wall. The tiger targeted a solitary cow resting alone. However, the other cows in the herd promptly rallied to their companion's aid. They closed in on the tiger, unitedly attacking the carnivore to drive it away. This display of solidarity among herbivores against a predator is rare. The tiger, unable to hunt any cattle from the herd, waited for about three hours before finally retreating. The injured cow is now under treatment, and its condition is reportedly critical. The 76-acre farm, equipped with 50 CCTV cameras, continues to witness tiger movements in the nearby hillocks. This heartwarming incident exemplifies how adversity can forge bonds and inspire collective courage among unlikely allies.

Dear reader, you too are a climber. Your Everest awaits—whether it's a career challenge, a broken heart, or a pandemic. Embrace the storms; they sculpt your character. Rise like a phoenix, for you are more than a conqueror. And remember, on this winding path, we're all legends in the making.

Resilience theory emphasizes that it's not the nature of adversity itself that matters most, but rather how we respond to it. When faced with misfortune, frustration, or challenges, resilience enables us to bounce back, survive, recover, and even thrive. It's a dynamic capacity that allows us to adapt successfully to life's difficulties.

In essence, resilience isn't about avoiding adversity; it's about embracing it as an opportunity for growth. By navigating adversity, we gain rich roots of character, courage, grace, and strength. Rather than interpreting adversity as weakness, we recognize it as a chance to develop virtues and build inner fortitude.

Whether in social work, family dynamics, or organizational contexts, resilience plays a crucial role in our ability to withstand life's storms and emerge stronger. It's a reminder that our responses matter, shaping our journey through adversity and ultimately defining our character.

RESILIENCE IS LEARNING TO DANCE IN THE RAIN.
EACH SETBACK IS A STEPPING STONE TO STRENGTH.

Chapter 6: Love and Relationships

Different forms of love - it's impact on our lives

Love is the invisible thread that weaves our existence into a meaningful tapestry. Its importance resonates across cultures, ages, and experiences. Love nourishes our emotional well-being. Whether it's the warmth of family bonds, the laughter shared with friends, or the passion of romantic connections, love provides a sense of belonging and purpose. Scientifically, love has a positive impact on our health. It reduces stress, lowers blood pressure, and boosts our immune system. When we feel loved, our bodies respond with resilience.

Love teaches us empathy—to understand and share the feelings of others. It encourages compassion, kindness, and selflessness. When we love, we become better versions of ourselves. Love fuels our aspirations. Whether it's the love for a hobby, a cause, or a person, it drives us to create, achieve, and persevere. Love ignites our inner fire. Love bridges gaps. It connects hearts across distances, cultures, and backgrounds. In times of joy or sorrow, love provides unwavering support—a shoulder to lean on, a hand to hold.

Love leaves imprints. The love we give and receive becomes our legacy. It lives on in stories, photographs, and cherished memories. Love transcends time. Love touches the soul. It's the essence of spiritual teachings—the love for humanity, nature, and the divine. Love connects us to something greater than ourselves.

In the grand symphony of life, love is the melody that lingers, the harmony that resonates. Cherish it, nurture it, and let it colour your days. Love, in all its multifaceted glory, weaves intricate threads through our lives, shaping our experiences, connections, and emotions. Let's delve into the various forms of love and their profound impact:

1. Romantic Love

Romantic love is the stuff of poetry, songs, and starry-eyed gazes. It's the passionate fire that ignites between partners, the magnetic pull that draws souls together. Here are its defining features:

Intense Attraction: Romantic love is characterized by intense physical and emotional attraction. It's the butterflies in your stomach, the longing for closeness, and the desire to share your life with someone.

Physical Intimacy: Unlike other forms of love, romantic love often involves physical intimacy—holding hands, stolen kisses, and shared warmth beneath cozy blankets.

Commitment: Romantic love isn't just about infatuation; it's also about commitment. It's the promise to weather storms together, to be each other's safe harbour.

Love at First Sight: Two teenagers, Alex and Mia, crossed paths in a bustling bookstore. Their eyes met over a stack of old love letters, and in that moment, time stood still. Alex's heart raced as he stumbled over his words, asking Mia about her favourite book. Mia blushed, and they exchanged numbers. Their love story unfolded through late-night texts, shared playlists, and stolen glances. It was a symphony of firsts—the first touch, the first kiss, and the first "I love you."

The Forgotten Diary: Ella, an antique store owner, discovered an old leather-bound diary tucked away in a dusty corner. The pages revealed the passionate love story of Liam and Isabella, separated by war. Through ink-stained words, Ella felt their longing, their stolen moments, and their promises. Determined to reunite their souls, Ella embarked on a quest to find Liam, guided by the echoes of love that transcended time.

The Café Serendipity: Lucas, a struggling writer, frequented a cozy café where he found solace in his coffee cup and the view of the park. One rainy afternoon, Sophia stumbled in, drenched and dishevelled. Their eyes met, and Lucas offered her his umbrella. They shared stories—their dreams, their fears, and their favourite poems. The café became their sanctuary, where love brewed like freshly ground coffee beans.

The Midnight Train: Olivia boarded the midnight train to escape her monotonous life. Across the aisle sat Henry, a musician with a guitar and a heartache. As the train chugged through moonlit landscapes, they shared secrets—the kind that only strangers reveal. Henry strummed his guitar, and Olivia hummed along. Their melodies merged, creating a love song that echoed through the night. When the train reached its final stop, they knew it was just the beginning.

The Star-Crossed Photograph: Emma, a photographer, stumbled upon an old photo in an antique shop. It captured a couple dancing under a starlit sky. The inscription read: Daniel and Eleanor, 1945. Emma became obsessed with their story. She researched archives, interviewed locals, and pieced together their lives. Daniel was a soldier, and Eleanor was a nurse. Their love bloomed amidst wartime chaos—a love that defied distance, fear, and time itself.

The Language of Flowers: Nina, a florist, believed in the secret language of blooms. When Ethan walked into her shop, she noticed the way he lingered near the roses— the symbol of love. Nina crafted a bouquet with red roses, white lilies (for purity), and forget-me-nots (for eternal love). Ethan blushed as he accepted the flowers. Their love story unfolded through petals—a silent confession that blossomed into forever.

2. Platonic Love

Platonic love blooms in friendships and familial bonds. It's the steady flame that warms our hearts without the heat of passion. Here's what you need to know:

Deep Connection: Platonic love is about emotional connection, trust, and shared experiences. It's the friend who knows your secrets and stands by you through thick and thin.

No Romantic Attraction: Unlike romantic love, platonic love doesn't involve sexual attraction. It's the love you feel for your best friend, your confidante, or your sibling.

Enduring Bonds: Platonic love often lasts a lifetime. Friends become family, and their impact on our lives is immeasurable.

The Unbreakable Bond: In a small coastal town, two childhood friends, Alex and Maya, shared an unbreakable bond. They spent countless hours exploring hidden coves, collecting seashells, and dreaming about their futures. As they grew older, their connection deepened. When life threw storms their way, they stood by each other, unwavering. Their love was platonic yet stronger than any tempest that came their way.

The Art of Letters: Emily and Daniel were pen pals separated by oceans. Their letters traveled across continents, carrying their hopes, dreams, and fears. They shared secrets, celebrated victories, and consoled each other during heartaches. Their words painted a canvas of platonic intimacy—a masterpiece of understanding, vulnerability, and unwritten promises.

The Midnight Ritual: Every full moon, Lily and James met at the old oak tree in the park. They sat side by side, gazing at the moon, and whispered their deepest thoughts. Lily confided her fears of failure, while James revealed his longing for adventure. Their platonic connection transcended time, and the moon became their silent witness to a bond that needed no labels.

The Library Chronicles: Sarah and Mark frequented the same library. They bonded over shared book recommendations, literary debates, and late-night discussions. Their platonic love was woven into the pages of novels—their hearts bookmarked by passages that mirrored their souls. When Mark moved away, Sarah sent him a handwritten letter: "Our friendship is a novel I'll reread forever."

The Symphony of Friendship: Rachel played the violin, and David was a pianist. Their music echoed through the empty concert hall during late-night rehearsals. Their notes harmonized, creating a symphony of platonic love. When Rachel lost her father, David sat beside her, playing a melancholic melody that spoke of shared grief and unwavering support. Their bond transcended applause and standing ovations.

The Garden of Trust: In the community garden, Maria and Carlos tended to their plants. Maria's sunflowers stood tall, while Carlos nurtured delicate orchids. They exchanged gardening tips, but their conversations went deeper. Maria confessed her fear of abandonment, and Carlos shared his struggle with anxiety. Their platonic love blossomed like the flowers they cared for—a sanctuary of trust and vulnerability.

The Starry Nights: On clear nights, Ava and Liam lay on the grass, staring at the constellations. They traced imaginary lines between stars, creating their own celestial patterns. Ava whispered her dreams of exploring the universe, while Liam talked about his love for astrophysics. Their platonic connection was written in stardust—a cosmic bond that defied gravity.

3. Familial Love

Familial love, often referred to as storge, is like a warm, cozy blanket that wraps around family members. It's the kind of love that doesn't need grand gestures or fancy words. Instead, it thrives on everyday moments: a shared meal, a bedtime story, or a comforting hug. Parents cheer for their kids at soccer games, siblings bicker over the TV remote, and grandparents tell tales of their youth. It's a love that grows roots deep into our hearts, connecting us across generations. It's the late-night lullabies sung by tired moms, the scraped knees kissed by concerned dads, and the shared laughter during family game nights. Parents pour their hearts into nurturing their little ones, while children find safety and acceptance in their parents' arms. It's the whispered "I love you" before bedtime, the comforting presence during thunderstorms, and the unwavering support through life's ups and downs. In this beautiful dance of love, parents teach their children to walk, and children teach their parents to see the world anew. Familial love is the bedrock of our existence. It's the love we inherit, the ties that bind us to parents, siblings, and extended family. Here's why it matters:

Unconditional: Familial love is unwavering. It's the love that forgives, supports, and sacrifices. It's the late-night conversations with your mom, the shared laughter with your cousins, and the protective instincts of a big brother.

Rooted in History: Our family shapes our identity. Whether through genetics or shared memories, familial love grounds us and gives us a sense of belonging.

Legacy of Love: From bedtime stories to family recipes, familial love leaves an indelible mark. It's the love that echoes through generations.

Reunited in Goa: In the heart of Goa, three generations of a family gather for a reunion. Amidst the sun-kissed beaches and swaying palm trees, they share laughter, memories, and secrets. The salty breeze carries their love—a love that transcends time and distance. As the sun sets, they realize that family is not just blood; it's the warmth that wraps around you when life's waves threaten to pull you under.

A Grandfather's Treasured Legacy: In a cozy Mangalorean home, young Ravi listens to his grandfather's tales. The old man's eyes sparkle as he recounts his adventures—the spice trade, monsoons at sea, and lost love. But it's not the stories alone that bind them; it's the legacy of resilience, courage, and love passed down through generations. Ravi learns that family history is etched not in books, but in the wrinkles of a beloved face.

Ties That Bind: A father and son embark on a road trip. The open highway stretches before them, and with each mile, their conversations deepen. They talk about dreams, heartaches, and the constellations above. The car becomes a cocoon of shared experiences, where love is the fuel that propels them forward. As they reach their destination, they realize that the journey mattered more than the destination itself.

Beating Depression Through Brother-Sister Bonding: When Maya's world turns grey, her younger brother Arjun becomes her lifeline. He listens without judgment, shares silly jokes, and reminds her of sunrises after the darkest nights. Their bond becomes her anchor, pulling her out of the abyss. In Arjun's laughter, Maya finds hope, and in his hugs, she discovers healing. Sometimes, love wears the face of a sibling who refuses to let you down.

Tea Time: Every evening, Mrs. Kapoor brews a pot of masala chai. The aroma fills the house, drawing her children and grandchildren to the kitchen. As they sip the spiced tea, they share snippets of their day—triumphs, heartaches, and mundane joys. The teacups become vessels of love, and the clinking of spoons against porcelain echoes the rhythm of their intertwined lives. In that simple act of tea-making, Mrs. Kapoor weaves her family together.

4. Self-Love

Self-love is the quiet revolution within. It's the acceptance of our flaws, the celebration of our strengths, and the nurturing of our well-being. Here's why it matters:

Inner Compass: Self-love guides us toward self-care. It's the permission to prioritize ourselves, set boundaries, and practice kindness toward our own hearts.

Resilience: When we love ourselves, we become resilient. We bounce back from setbacks, embrace imperfections, and find joy in our uniqueness.

Foundation for Other Loves: Loving ourselves allows us to love others more authentically. It's the oxygen mask we put on first before helping others.

In the grand tapestry of life, these forms of love interweave, creating a rich and colourful mosaic. They impact our choices, our happiness, and our very essence. So, let's celebrate love in all its forms—whether whispered in moonlight gardens or shared over a cup of tea with an old friend.

IN THE SYMPHONY OF EXISTENCE,
LOVE PLAYS VARIED MELODIES.

Chapter 7: Purpose and Passion

Life meaning | Discover the purpose | Passion driving us forward

Purpose is the compass that guides our actions, decisions, and aspirations. It gives meaning to our existence and fuels our journey. Purpose refers to the reason or intention behind our actions, endeavours, and existence. It is the driving force that propels us forward, motivating us to pursue specific goals and objectives. Whether it's a company aiming to increase profits or an individual seeking personal growth, purpose provides direction and clarity. Our purpose can be short-term or long-term, evolving as circumstances change and priorities shift.

On the other hand, significance encompasses the importance and meaning attached to something. It measures the impact an action or event has on individuals, organizations, or society as a whole. Significance goes beyond the immediate outcome; it involves a broader perspective and a deeper understanding of implications. For instance, a scientific discovery may hold significant implications for medicine, while a social movement can profoundly impact culture and values. Significance is subjective, varying based on context and individual perspective.

These two concepts are intertwined: purpose gives us direction and motivation, while significance infuses our lives with meaning and value. When we align our purpose with actions that hold significance, we create a fulfilling existence. So, let's reflect on our purpose, recognize our significance, and live intentionally, knowing that both aspects contribute to a richer, more purposeful life.

Purpose - The Guiding Compass: Purpose is like a trusty compass that accompanies us on life's grand adventure. It's the North Star that illuminates our path, making our journey meaningful and exciting. Imagine purpose as the spark that ignites our passions and fuels our dreams. Whether we're chasing career goals, embarking on personal quests, or simply savouring everyday moments, purpose whispers, "This way, my friend!" It's the reason we leap out of bed in the morning, ready to conquer the day.

Purpose in Action: Think of purpose as the secret sauce that flavours our decisions. When a company sets out to create innovative products, it's fuelled by purpose—the desire to make a difference. And you, dear individual, seeking personal growth? Your purpose might be as simple as learning a new skill or as profound as leaving a positive impact on the world. Purpose isn't a rigid blueprint; it's a flexible roadmap that adapts as life swirls around us. Short-term or long-term, it dances with our evolving priorities, nudging us towards fulfilment.

Significance: The Ripple Effect Now, let's meet its partner in crime: significance. Picture significance as a pebble dropped into a tranquil pond. The ripples spread far beyond the initial splash. When we act with purpose, our deeds gain significance. It's not just about ticking off tasks; it's about creating waves of impact. A scientific discovery? Oh, it can revolutionize medicine, touching lives we'll never meet. And that social movement? It reshapes culture, nudging humanity toward empathy and progress. Significance isn't a solo act; it's a symphony of interconnected nodes.

Purpose + Significance = Magic: These two concepts waltz together under the moonlight. Purpose gives us direction—like a mischievous breeze guiding a paper airplane. It nudges us toward our goals, whispering, "You've got this!" But significance? Ah, it sprinkles stardust on our existence. When we align purpose with actions that matter, we create magic. It's the joy of mentoring a budding artist, the warmth of volunteering at a shelter, or the thrill of solving a complex puzzle. Purpose and significance high-five, creating a richer, more purposeful life.

Reflection Time: So, my friend, let's sip metaphorical tea and reflect. What's your purpose? What tiny or colossal significance can you sprinkle into the world? As you live intentionally, remember that both purpose and significance are your trusty companions. They'll hold your hand through sunrises and storms, weaving a tapestry of memories.

The Power of Passion

Passion ignites the fire within us. It's the force that propels us forward, even when challenges arise. Passion is like a sparkly magic potion that makes life exciting! Imagine it as the secret ingredient that turns ordinary days into extraordinary adventures. Fuel for Will: John Maxwell, a renowned motivational speaker and leadership author, aptly describes passion as "the fuel for will." When we're passionate, mere obligations morph into fervent desires. We shift from "have-to's" to "want-to's." The intensity of our longing propels us forward, unyielding in our pursuit. Life coach Jan Gordon defines passion as the essence of commitment. It's the fire that stirs us from within, motivating our actions. Without passion, our endeavours lack meaning; results remain elusive. Passion is the seed from which commitment blossoms—a force that compels us to persist despite obstacles. Pursuing passion isn't always straightforward. While some lucky souls stumble upon their life's calling effortlessly, most of us must carve out time amidst our busy lives. Patience, hard work, and persistence are our allies. Whether it aligns with a career or a personal cause, passion demands effort. Passion extends beyond our professional lives. If you're passionate about feeding the hungry or aiding the homeless, it needn't be your job. Commitment lies in finding opportunities to contribute. In our overscheduled world, making time for what we love isn't easy, but it's undeniably worthwhile.

Creativity: Passion acts as a catalyst for creativity. When you're passionate about something, your mind becomes a fertile ground for innovative ideas. It's as if your imagination sprouts wings, allowing you to explore uncharted territories. Fresh perspectives emerge, and you find unique solutions to challenges. Passion ignites the spark of creativity, turning ordinary thoughts into extraordinary innovations.

Resilience: Passion provides the resilience needed to weather life's storms. It's the unwavering force that keeps you moving forward, even when faced with seemingly insurmountable obstacles. Passionate individuals bounce back from setbacks because their commitment runs deep. They draw strength from their inner fire, refusing to be defeated. Resilience fuelled by passion transforms adversity into stepping stones toward growth.

Unwavering Commitment: Passionate people are like lighthouses in a storm. They don't give up easily. Their dedication to their goals remains steadfast, regardless of external circumstances. When challenges arise, they lean on their passion—the unwavering flame within—to guide them.

Not Always a Smooth Ride: Pursuing passion isn't always a walk in the park. Sometimes it's more like a jungle adventure. You'll need a machete (okay, maybe just determination) to clear the path. But guess what? The wild journey is where the magic happens.

Beyond Work: Passion isn't just about jobs. Maybe you're passionate about baking cookies, saving the environment, or mastering yo-yo tricks. Whatever it is, sprinkle passion into your life. Even if it's not your 9-to-5 gig, it's worth every second.

Supercharge Your Dreams: Passion is like turbo boosters for your dreams. When you're passionate about something, it's not just a task—it's an exciting quest! Suddenly, you're not dragging yourself; you're zooming toward your goals with a grin on your face.

Three Feet away from Gold: During the gold rush, a man had been tirelessly mining in Colorado for several months. Frustrated by the lack of success, he quit his job and sold his equipment. Another miner took over where he left off. The new miner consulted an engineer who revealed that there was gold just three feet away from where the first miner had stopped digging. The first miner had been incredibly close to striking gold before giving up.

Moral: When faced with adversity, persevere. Often, success is closer than it seems, and pushing a little harder can lead to victory.

Rocks, Pebbles, and Sand: A philosophy professor demonstrated a lesson to his class using a large empty mayonnaise jar. He filled it with large rocks and asked if it was full. The students agreed. Then he added small pebbles, which filled the gaps between the rocks. Again, he asked if the jar was full, and the students hesitantly agreed. Finally, he poured in sand, which filled the remaining spaces. The jar was truly full.

Moral: Prioritize what truly matters (the big rocks) and fit in the smaller tasks (pebbles and sand) around them. Passionate pursuit of your core goals will help you achieve fulfilment.

The Power of Passion in Real Lives: Malala Yousafzai, the Nobel laureate and education activist, risked her life to advocate for girls' education in Pakistan. Elon Musk, the entrepreneur and innovator, relentlessly pursues his vision for sustainable energy and space exploration. Serena Williams, the tennis champion, exemplifies passion through her dedication to her craft and her resilience in overcoming challenges.

Moral: Passion fuels extraordinary achievements. When you wholeheartedly pursue what you love, you can create lasting impact and inspire others.

Aligning Purpose and Passion

Imagine a painter, standing before a blank canvas, their heart brimming with hues waiting to burst forth. They dip their brush into vibrant pigments—the reds of sunrise, the blues of endless skies, the yellows of hope—and they weave them into a mural that stretches across a weathered wall. This isn't just art; it's a beacon of resilience for a struggling community. Each stroke whispers stories of courage, whispers of dreams, and whispers of healing. The painter's passion for colours dances with purpose—to uplift hearts, to ignite hope, and to transform spaces that were once barren into sanctuaries of possibility.

Now shift your gaze to a classroom—a place where curiosity blooms like wildflowers after rain. There stands a teacher, their eyes alight with wonder. They hold a magnifying glass, revealing the intricate patterns on a butterfly's wing. Their voice, a symphony of enthusiasm, narrates the wonders of photosynthesis, the magic of chemical reactions, and the mysteries of the cosmos. This teacher isn't merely imparting knowledge; they're nurturing minds, planting seeds of curiosity that will sprout into future scientists, explorers, and dreamers. Their passion for education pirouettes gracefully alongside their purpose—to ignite the flames of inquiry, to guide young minds toward discovery, and to shape a world where questions are celebrated.

Passion and purpose—they intertwine like vines, each supporting the other. But they're not static; they're a dance. Sometimes, the steps are fluid—a waltz across sun-kissed meadows, where passion and purpose twirl in harmony. Other times, they stumble—a tango on uneven ground, where doubts creep in, and the rhythm falters. Yet with each misstep, there's growth. With each twirl, there's self-discovery. The painter learns that their purpose extends beyond aesthetics—it's a lifeline for hearts that ache. The teacher realizes that their passion isn't confined to textbooks—it's a torch that illuminates the path of future explorers.

So, my friend, keep dancing. When passion and purpose align, the heart becomes a compass, pointing toward fulfilment. Let your purpose be the North Star, unwavering and true. Let your passion be the wind that propels you forward. And in this grand ballroom of existence, let your heart lead the way—through graceful turns and stumbling spins—until you find that sweet spot where your soul sings, and the dance becomes a symphony of purposeful living.

Living with Purpose and Passion

Passion isn't a luxury; it's oxygen for the spirit. Whether it's the scientist poring over equations, the musician lost in melodies, or the gardener tending to blossom, passion infuses life with vitality. It's the heartbeat of existence, reminding us that we're more than cogs in a machine.

But purpose and passion aren't solitary travellers; they waltz together. Purpose lends depth to passion—it transforms a hobby into a calling, a job into a mission.

When we align our actions with our core values, purpose blooms. And passion fuels purpose—it propels us forward when obstacles loom, infusing our endeavours with resilience.

Living with purpose and passion means daring to dream audaciously. It's about finding the sweet spot where our heart's desires intersect with the world's needs. It's the teacher who kindles curiosity, the artist who paints hope, the entrepreneur who builds bridges. It's the nurse who tends to wound, the poet who weaves verses, the parent who shapes futures. Each act, no matter how small, becomes a brushstroke—a stroke that colours the canvas of our days.

Yet, this dance isn't always graceful. There are stumbling steps, moments of doubt, and seasons of uncertainty. But therein lies growth—the messy, beautiful evolution. Purpose evolves as we learn, adapt, and redefine. Passion deepens as we explore new avenues, as we fall and rise again. And in this dance, we discover facets of ourselves— the resilient, the compassionate, the relentless dreamer.

So, my friend, embrace the rhythm. Seek purpose with intention, but don't forget to chase fireflies of passion. Let your heart lead, and let your days be a symphony—a harmonious blend of purposeful strides and passionate leaps. For in this dance, we find not just existence, but a life that sings—a life that whispers, "You matter."

Let's delve deeper into living with purpose and passion.

1. Self-Reflection and Exploration:

Begin by creating a quiet space for introspection. Reflect on your life journey—the highs, lows, and pivotal moments. What experiences have shaped you? What values resonate with your core? Self-awareness is the compass that guides you toward passion and purpose. Explore various interests. Engage in activities that intrigue you. Attend workshops, read books, and immerse yourself in different domains. Passion often reveals itself when you're fully engaged and lose track of time.

2. Passion: The Fire Within:

Passion isn't a fleeting emotion; it's an inner fire that fuels your actions. It's the joy you feel when you're immersed in something you love. Identify your passions—whether it's writing, dancing, cooking, or solving complex problems. Passionate pursuits light up your soul. Ask yourself: "What activities make my heart race? When do I feel most alive?" These clues lead you to your passions.

3. Purpose: Your North Star:

Purpose transcends personal desires. It's about contributing to a larger whole. Consider your unique gifts and strengths. How can they serve others or the world?

Purpose gives life meaning beyond individual fulfilment. Reflect on questions like: "What impact do I want to make? How can I leave the world better than I found it?"

4. The Dance of Alignment:

Aligning passion and purpose is like choreographing a beautiful dance. Passion provides the energy; purpose provides the direction. Imagine a ballet dancer—passion fuels the graceful movements; purpose ensures they stay on stage. Explore how your passions intersect with meaningful causes. For instance, if you love photography, use it to raise awareness about environmental conservation.

5. Living with Conviction:

Purposeful living requires commitment. Set clear intentions. Write down your purpose statement. It needn't be grand; it can be as simple as "I want to inspire kindness." Infuse passion into your daily life. If you're passionate about education, mentor someone. If you love gardening, create a community garden. Purposeful actions ripple outward.

6. Overcoming Challenges:

Challenges test your resolve. Passion keeps you going, purpose gives you resilience. When obstacles arise, remind yourself why you're on this path. Purpose fuels determination. Remember, even setbacks contribute to your growth. They refine your purpose.

7. Community and Connection:

Surround yourself with like-minded souls. Connect with people who share your passions and purpose. Attend meetups, join online forums, and collaborate. Collective energy amplifies impact. Share your journey. Vulnerability inspires others.

8. Celebrate Progress:

Celebrate milestones. Whether it's completing a project, volunteering, or learning a new skill, acknowledge your progress. Gratitude magnifies passion. Each step taken with purpose is a victory.

9. Review and Adjust the Sails:

Regularly assess your alignment. Are you living authentically? Adjust as needed. Purpose evolves as you do. Be open to redirection. Remember, purpose isn't static—it's a dynamic force that grows with you.

10. Legacy and Fulfilment:

Imagine your life as a canvas. What legacy do you want to paint? Purposeful living leaves brushstrokes of impact. Whether it's nurturing relationships, creating art, or advocating for change, your purpose matters. Fulfilment lies in knowing you've lived with passion and left footprints of purpose.

The art of overcoming challenges while living with purpose and passion:

Living with passion and purpose is akin to harnessing an inner fire that propels us forward, even in the face of adversity. It's about embracing life with unwavering commitment, fuelled by a vision that aligns with our core values, strengths, and talents. Challenges are inevitable, but when we live with passion, we transform obstacles into stepping stones. Passion emerges from both love and pain, driving us to make a positive difference. It's the energy that empowers us to overcome fear, indecision, and procrastination. When pursuing our passions, we venture beyond comfort zones, seeking experiences that ignite our souls. So, let us embrace the art of living purposefully, fuelled by the flames of passion, as we navigate life's unpredictable terrain.

- **Embrace the Journey:** Living with purpose and passion is akin to embarking on a grand adventure. It's not a static state but a dynamic process. Embrace the journey, even when it takes unexpected turns. Challenges are part of this expedition—they test your resolve and reveal your true character. Rather than fearing them, view challenges as opportunities for growth.
- **Purpose as Your North Star:** Purpose provides direction. It's the North Star guiding your decisions, actions, and aspirations. When faced with challenges, remind yourself of your purpose. Why are you here? What impact do you want to make? Purpose fuels determination and resilience. It's the anchor that keeps you steady during life's storms.

- **Passion as Your Fuel:** Passion is the fire that burns within. It's the force that propels you forward, even when exhaustion threatens to engulf you. Passionate individuals don't merely survive; they thrive. When challenges arise, tap into your passion. Reconnect with what sets your soul ablaze. Passionate people don't give up easily; they find creative solutions and forge ahead.

- **Mindset Matters: Challenges often trigger negative thoughts:** "I can't do this," "It's too hard," or "I'm not good enough." Shift your mindset. Instead of seeing obstacles as roadblocks, view them as stepping stones. Each challenge is an opportunity to learn, adapt, and evolve. Cultivate a growth mindset—one that embraces setbacks as valuable lessons.

- **Resilience and Adaptability:** Purposeful living requires resilience. When faced with adversity, bounce back. Adaptability is your superpower. Consider bamboo—it bends with the wind but doesn't break. Similarly, adapt to changing circumstances without compromising your purpose. Resilience isn't about avoiding challenges; it's about thriving despite them.

- **Learn from Setbacks:** Challenges aren't failures; they're feedback. When you stumble, pause and reflect. What can you learn? How can you improve? Use setbacks as stepping stones to success. Thomas Edison didn't see his 1,000 failed attempts at creating the light bulb as failures; he saw them as discoveries of what didn't work. Learn, adjust, and persevere.

- **Community and Support:** You're not alone in this journey. Surround yourself with like-minded individuals who share your passion and purpose. Seek mentors, friends, and allies who uplift you during tough times. Community provides encouragement, fresh perspectives, and collaborative solutions. Together, you can overcome even the most daunting challenges.

- **Celebrate Small Wins:** Purposeful living isn't about waiting for grand victories. Celebrate small wins—the moments when you pushed through fear, took a step forward, or learned something new. These mini triumphs build momentum. They remind you that progress is happening, even if it's gradual. Celebrate your resilience and progress.

Let's sprinkle some friendly magic into our exploration of inspiring others to live with passion and purpose.

Build Up Those Around You:

High-Five Moments: Imagine you're at a celebration, and someone just aced a task. Give them a virtual high-five! Acknowledge their efforts, whether it's a well-prepared meal or a beautifully crafted spreadsheet. Your encouragement fuels their motivation. Be the cheerleader of everyday victories. When someone conquers a fear or completes a project, cheer them on. It's like sprinkling confetti on their path!

Be Enthusiastic:

Picture this: You're excited about a new hobby or a weekend adventure. Share that joy! Enthusiasm is like a catchy tune; it gets stuck in people's heads. Dance through life, and others might join your groove. When you're passionate about something—be it gardening, solving puzzles, or baking cookies—invite others to your show-and-tell. Their curiosity might ignite their own passions.

Have Integrity: Integrity isn't about being perfect; it's about being consistent. Imagine you're the captain of the "S.S. Authenticity." Sail through life with unwavering honesty. Others will want to hop aboard. Integrity bakes trust cookies. When you keep your promises and stay true to your values, you're handing out warm, chocolate-chip trust cookies. People love those!

Practice Empathy: Imagine you're sitting with a friend who's having a tough day. Listen with your heart. Sometimes, all they need is a compassionate ear. Empathy is like a cozy blanket—it wraps people in warmth. When you show kindness, it sets off a chain reaction. Imagine kindness as colourful dominoes. Tip one and watch the rest fall into place.

Maintain a Positive Outlook: Put on your metaphorical sunshine glasses. Even when clouds gather, look for silver linings. Share stories of overcoming storms. Your optimism becomes a pocket-sized sunbeam. Imagine hope as tiny seeds. Scatter them everywhere. When you say, "We'll figure this out," you're planting hope seeds. They sprout courage.

Express Gratitude: Imagine you have a magical gratitude journal. Write down moments that made your heart smile. Share them! Gratitude is like a secret handshake—it connects hearts. When someone helps you out, send them a mental bouquet of thank-you. Imagine it blooming in their inbox. Gratitude bridges gaps.

Stand Your Ground: Imagine you're a brave knight defending a castle (your beliefs). When dragons of doubt or peer pressure approach, draw your sword (metaphorically). Others will see your courage and polish their armour too. Life serves resilience cookies. They're chewy and tough, but they make us stronger. Share your cookie jar—tell stories of bouncing back. Others will grab a cookie and keep going.

Set Clear Goals: Imagine your purpose as a treasure map. Draw it with colourful markers. Share your map! Others might find their own buried treasures. Goal setting is like a compass—it points the way. Invite others on your goal-setting adventure. Imagine you're hiking up a mountain. When someone joins your trail, it becomes a team expedition.

Lead by Example: Imagine your passions as fireworks. Light them up! Whether it's painting, coding, or salsa dancing, let your sparks fly. Others will watch in awe and think, "I want my own fireworks show!" Imagine you're walking on a sandy beach. Your footprints leave a trail. Be authentic, and others will follow your beachcomber path.

Connect with Strengths: Imagine talents as seeds. Sprinkle them generously. Encourage others to explore their unique abilities. When they bloom, it's like a garden is partying to celebrate growth. Host a passion potluck! Everyone brings their favourite dish of enthusiasm. Imagine the flavours—music, gardening, stargazing. Share and savour.

Life is like a cosmic playground, where we swing on sunbeams and slide down rainbows. Our purpose? It's like finding the perfect pebble to skip across the universe—a little adventure, a lot of joy. Passion is our secret sauce, sprinkled on morning pancakes and tucked into bedtime stories. It's the giggle in our stardust, the high-five with moonbeams. So, let's chase fireflies of curiosity, hug constellations, and share Milky Way smiles. Because life's recipe? Love, laughter, and a dash of wonder. We wander through meadows of possibility, Leaving footprints on stardust, our legacy. Purpose blooms in kindness shared, in laughter, in love—our souls bared.

The Musician's Gift In a bustling city: There lived an old street musician named Elias. His violin was weathered, its strings frayed, but when he played, magic flowed through the air. People hurried past, too busy to notice the melodies that painted the cobblestones. One day, a young girl named Maya stopped. Her eyes widened as Elias's fingers danced across the strings. She listened, captivated. Elias smiled, knowing he had found a kindred spirit. He whispered, "Passion is like music—it's meant to be shared." Inspired, Maya picked up her dusty guitar. She played in parks, hospitals, and crowded subway stations. Her music touched hearts, healing wounds and igniting dreams. Elias watched from afar, knowing his purpose was fulfilled—to awaken passion in others.

The Gardener's Legacy In a quaint village: There lived an elderly gardener named Mr. Patel. His garden was a riot of colours—roses, sunflowers, and daffodils. Children gathered to listen to his stories of soil, seasons, and resilience. When Mr. Patel passed away, the villagers mourned. But he had left a letter: "Plant seeds, my dear ones. Not just flowers, but dreams. Nurture them with love and purpose." Inspired, they transformed the village. Gardens bloomed, but so did schools, libraries, and community centres. Today, children play in Mr. Patel's Garden, their laughter echoing his legacy. They know that passion, like petals, unfurls when tended with care.

The Star Gazer's Quest Far from city lights, young Aria lay on the grass, gazing at the night sky. Her grandfather, an old astronomer, pointed out constellations—their stories etched in stardust. "Each star," he said, "holds a purpose. Find yours." Aria dreamed of exploring the cosmos. She studied physics, built telescopes, and launched rockets in her backyard. Years later, Aria stood at NASA, her heart racing. She'd designed a probe to explore distant planets. As it soared into space, she whispered, "Grandpa, I found my star." Back on Earth, children looked up, inspired by Aria's journey. They, too, dreamed of reaching for the stars.

LIFE
MEANING
DISCOVER THE MEANING, EMBRACE THE PURPOSE, AND LET THE
PASSION BE COMPASS THAT GUIDES TOWARDS YOUR TRUE NORTH.

Chapter 8: Lessons from Loss and Grief

Profound impact of loss—losing a loved one, a dream, or an opportunity

Grief is a universal human experience, transcending borders, cultures, and backgrounds. It is the emotional response to loss, whether it's the loss of a dream, the end of a relationship or the death of a loved one. While grief can be incredibly painful, it also offers profound lessons that shape our understanding of life and resilience. Here are some essential lessons we can learn from grief:

Grief Is a Healthy and Necessary Process

Grief is not something to be avoided or rushed through. It is a natural response to love lost, and it allows us to process our emotions, memories, and pain. Trying to suppress grief can lead to long-term emotional struggles. Instead, we should honour our grief and allow ourselves to feel it fully. Grief is a profound and essential process that accompanies loss. When we experience the pain of losing someone or something dear to us, grief becomes our companion. Grief allows us to recognize and express our emotions fully. It's healthy to feel sadness, anger, confusion, and even moments of relief. Suppressing these feelings can hinder healing. Through grief, we honour what was lost, a loved one, a dream, or an aspect of our identity. It's a way of paying tribute to the significance of what once existed. Grief doesn't follow a linear path. It comes in waves—sometimes crashing fiercely, other times gently lapping at our hearts. Patience is crucial as we ride these emotional tides. Our bodies respond to grief too. Tears, fatigue, changes in appetite, and disrupted sleep patterns are all part of the process. Listening to our bodies is essential. Grief isn't meant to be borne alone. Connecting with others who understand or seeking professional help can provide solace and guidance. Grief invites us to explore existential questions. We grapple with the purpose of life, the nature of existence, and our beliefs. This search for meaning is a vital part of healing. Beyond the primary loss, grief brings secondary losses—changes in relationships, roles, and routines. Recognizing and adapting to these shifts is essential. As we navigate grief, we discover our inner resilience. We learn to live with the void, find new ways to connect, and eventually grow from the experience. In essence, grief is a testament to our capacity to love deeply. It's a process that reshapes us, leaving imprints on our hearts—a mosaic of memories, tears, and eventual acceptance.

In a village surrounded by hills, an ancient oak tree stood tall. Its branches, like gnarled fingers, reached for the sky. Each autumn, it shed its leaves—a quiet mourning. "Why does the tree weep?" young Aria asked.

> The wise elder replied, "Grief, my child. It's like shedding leaves. Natural. Healing."
>
> As winter came, the tree stood bare. But within, roots held memories. Spring arrived, leaves sprouted, and hope bloomed.
>
> And so, the old oak taught: Grief is resilience. Love is stored and remembered.

Loss Is Inevitable

Grief is like a gentle tap on our shoulder, whispering, "Hey, life is fleeting." We all go through tough moments—losing a family member, saying goodbye to a job, or watching a friendship fade away. But guess what? These experiences connect us as humans.

Acceptance of this inevitable truth becomes our compass. It guides us toward a deeper understanding of our own fragility and the transient nature of everything we hold dear. As we navigate the labyrinth of emotions, we learn to appreciate the present moment—the sun's warmth on our skin, the laughter shared over a cup of coffee, the fleeting touch of a loved one's hand. Each connection, no matter how brief, becomes a precious gem in the mosaic of our lives.

Grief, paradoxically, becomes a testament to our capacity for love and resilience. It carves out space within us, allowing us to hold both joy and sorrow simultaneously.

And in this delicate balance, we find solace—a reminder that our hearts are vast enough to cradle both memories and hope. So, let us honour our losses, for they illuminate the contours of our humanity, and let us cherish our connections, knowing that they are the constellations that guide us through the night.

The Fallen Leaf: Once upon a time, in a large forest, there was a tall, beautiful tree. It was home to a vibrant leaf that was the envy of all others. The leaf was proud of its lush green color and lofty position. But as the seasons changed, so did the leaf. It turned from green to yellow, then from yellow to red. Despite its efforts to cling to the branch, it eventually fell to the ground. The leaf had to accept that loss was a part of life, a cycle that every living being must go through.

The Sandcastle: A little boy spent hours building a beautiful sandcastle near the shore. He decorated it with shells and was very proud of his creation. However, as the tide came in, his sandcastle was washed away. The boy was upset, but his father comforted him, explaining that loss is inevitable. Everything we build or acquire in this world is temporary.

The Farmer's Crop: A farmer worked tirelessly on his fields, sowing seeds and tending to his crops. He was looking forward to a bountiful harvest. However, a severe storm destroyed his crops just before the harvest season. The farmer was devastated but realized that loss is a part of life. He learned to accept the loss and prepared to sow seeds for the next season.

Cherish Loved Ones

Grief often comes with the realization that we may not have appreciated our loved ones as much as we could have when they were with us. This understanding can lead us to not take the presence of our loved ones for granted in the future. We learn to cherish every moment we have with them, knowing that these moments are fleeting. Grief can also teach us the importance of expressing our feelings. Often, we regret the words left unsaid more than the ones we spoke. Grief encourages us to express love, gratitude, and other emotions to our loved ones while we still have the opportunity. It teaches us that it's important to say "I love you," "I appreciate you," or "I forgive you," when we have the chance. The pain of loss can underscore the importance of spending quality time with those we care about. It's not just about being physically present, but also about being emotionally available, engaged, and invested in the moments we share with others. These shared experiences can create lasting memories that we can cherish long after our loved ones are gone. When we understand that any interaction might be our last, every conversation, every shared meal, every laugh, every shared silence becomes precious. We learn to be fully present in these moments, soaking in the joy, the love, and even the ordinary tranquillity they bring.

Patience and Self-Compassion

Grief is not something that can be rushed. It's a process that unfolds in its own time. Everyone experiences grief differently and on their own timeline. Some people may find that their grief lessens over weeks or months, while others may take years. It's important to allow ourselves the time we need to grieve. Grief often comes in waves, sometimes when we least expect it. One moment we might feel okay, and the next we might be overwhelmed with sadness. This is a normal part of the grieving process. It's important to be patient with ourselves as we navigate these waves of sorrow. Self-compassion involves treating ourselves with kindness, especially when we're struggling with painful emotions. It means acknowledging that it's okay to feel pain, to cry, and to struggle. It's about giving ourselves permission to be human and to experience the full range of human emotions. Healing from grief doesn't follow a straight line. It's not a matter of moving from point A (grief) to point B (healing) in a direct path. Instead, healing is often a messy, nonlinear journey. We might have good days and bad days. We might take two steps forward, then one step back. This is all part of the healing process. There's no right or wrong way to grieve, and there's no timeline for when we should be "over" our grief. The most important thing is to be patient and compassionate with ourselves as we navigate this difficult journey.

Secondary Losses

Beyond the primary loss, grief brings secondary losses. The dynamics of our relationships with others may change. Friends and family may not know how to respond to our grief, leading them to distance themselves. We may feel isolated or misunderstood. If the person we lost played a significant role in our lives (such as a parent, spouse, or child), their absence means we have to adjust to new roles. For example, a person who loses a spouse may have to take on tasks the spouse used to handle. Our sense of self can be tied up in our relationship with the person we lost. When they're gone, we may struggle with questions like "Who am I now?" or "What's my purpose?" Recognizing these secondary losses is an important part of the grieving process. It allows us to fully understand the impact of our loss and helps us adapt to our new reality. It also helps us find new ways to connect with others, perhaps by seeking support from those who've had similar experiences or by finding new activities that help us feel connected and fulfilled.

Grief and Joy Coexist

It's possible to experience joy even amidst grief. Laughter, beauty, and moments of connection can coexist with sadness. Embracing both emotions allows us to honour our pain while celebrating life's small victories.

"It's possible to experience joy even amidst grief." This means that even in times of deep sorrow or loss, moments of happiness can still occur. It could be a fond memory that brings a smile, a kind word from a friend, or simply a beautiful sunset. These moments of joy do not negate the grief, but they can exist alongside it, providing a counterpoint to the sorrow.

"Laughter, beauty, and moments of connection can coexist with sadness." This part of the statement is emphasizing that positive experiences (like laughter, appreciating beauty, or feeling connected to others) and negative emotions (like sadness) are not mutually exclusive. They can happen at the same time. For example, you might feel sad on the anniversary of a loved one's death, but also find joy in reminiscing about happy times you spent together.

"Embracing both emotions allows us to honour our pain while celebrating life's small victories." This suggests that by acknowledging and accepting our full range of emotions, we can navigate through difficult times more effectively. Honouring our pain means acknowledging our feelings of loss or sadness rather than denying them. At the same time, celebrating life's small victories means recognizing and appreciating the good moments that we encounter, no matter how small they may seem. This balance allows us to grieve while also continuing to engage with life.

In essence, this statement is about the human capacity for resilience and the ability to experience a wide range of emotions, even in challenging times. It's a reminder that it's okay to feel joy amidst sorrow, and that doing so can be a part of the healing process. It's a testament to the complexity and resilience of the human spirit.

The Empty Nest: Once upon a time, there was a mother bird who had spent her life caring for her chicks. She taught them to fly, to find food, and to sing. One by one, her chicks grew up and left the nest to start their own lives. The mother bird felt a deep sense of loss. Her nest, once filled with chirping and activity, was now silent and empty.

However, as she watched her chicks soar in the sky, she also felt a sense of joy. She was proud of the birds they had become and was happy to see them thriving. Even though she missed them terribly, she found joy in their independence and success.

The Lost Heirloom: A young woman named Maya had a necklace that was passed down through generations in her family. One day, she lost the necklace and was filled with grief. It was not just a piece of jewelry, but a symbol of her family's history and love.

Months later, while cleaning her house, Maya found the necklace in an unexpected place. The joy she felt was overwhelming. But along with the joy, there was also a sense of grief for the time she had spent believing it was lost. The coexistence of joy and grief made the moment of finding the necklace even more poignant.

Life Is Short and Unpredictable

"Grief reminds us that life can change in an instant." This means that the experience of grief often comes from a sudden loss or change, which serves as a stark reminder of the unpredictable nature of life. It underscores the reality that our circumstances can change dramatically and without warning. "We learn to appreciate each day, create meaningful experiences, and prioritize what truly matters." In the face of such unpredictability, we often find ourselves learning to value each day as it comes, recognizing that each moment is precious and not to be taken for granted. We strive to create experiences that are meaningful to us and those around us. We also learn to focus on what's truly important in our lives, often realizing that some things we once thought were crucial may not hold as much significance. "Seize opportunities, mend relationships, and live authentically." This part of the statement encourages us to take action in light of these realizations. "Seizing opportunities" means not waiting for the "right" moment to do something important or meaningful, but taking the initiative when the opportunity presents itself. "Mending relationships" suggests making an effort to repair broken or strained relationships, recognizing their value in our lives. "Living authentically" means being true to ourselves, our values, and our passions, rather than living according to others' expectations or societal pressures.

Memories Are Our Comfort "Memories of our loved ones become our solace." This means that when we lose someone we care about, our memories of them can provide comfort. These memories can be a source of peace and consolation, helping us cope with the loss. "They keep their presence alive within us." This suggests that through our memories, our loved ones continue to have a presence in our lives. Even though they are no longer physically with us, our memories keep them alive in our minds and hearts. "Whether through photographs, shared stories, or cherished objects, memories provide comfort and a sense of continuity." This part of the statement highlights different ways in which memories can be triggered or preserved. Photographs capture moments in time, shared stories keep personal experiences alive, and cherished objects can hold significant sentimental value. These tangible and intangible reminders help us remember our loved ones, providing comfort and a sense of ongoing connection. In essence, this statement is about the power of memory in dealing with loss. It's a reminder that even though someone may no longer be with us physically, they continue to live on in our memories and in the stories, photos, and objects they've left behind. These memories can provide comfort, a sense of continuity, and a way to keep our connection with our loved ones alive. It's a testament to the enduring impact of relationships and the healing power of remembrance.

Resilience Emerges

"Grief reveals our inner strength." This means that the process of grieving can often bring to light the strength we have within us. It's during these challenging times that we discover our capacity to endure, to heal, and to grow. "We survive the unimaginable, adapt to new realities, and find ways to honour our losses." This part of the statement speaks to the resilience of the human spirit. Despite experiencing loss that may seem unbearable, we find a way to continue living. We adapt to the new reality of our lives without the person or thing we've lost. Additionally, we find ways to honour our losses, perhaps through rituals, remembrance, or by living in a way that reflects their influence on our lives. "Resilience grows from the cracks of our broken hearts." This suggests that the very act of going through grief and coming out the other side makes us more resilient. Our hearts may be "broken" by the loss we've experienced, but it's through these "cracks" that our resilience grows. Just as a bone can become stronger after a break, our emotional resilience can strengthen after experiencing and healing from grief.

Remember that grief is not a linear process, and everyone experiences it uniquely. These lessons offer insights into our shared humanity and the transformative power of loss. May we learn, heal, and find meaning amid the pain.

IN THE HEARTACHE OF LOSS, WE DISCOVER THE STRENGTH TO GROW.
GRIEF IS NOT A ROADBLOCK, BUT A STEPPING STONE TO A WISDOM
THAT ENRICHES OUR SPIRIT.

Chapter 9: Time Management

Strategies for managing time effectively, setting priorities, and finding balance

Once upon a time, in a bustling city, there was a man named Joe. Joe was known for his brilliant mind and kind heart, but he had one flaw that often overshadowed his talents—his poor time management skills.

Joe worked at a tech startup, a place where deadlines were as frequent as the morning coffee. Despite his expertise, Joe's inability to manage his time well often led to missed deadlines and frustrated colleagues. He would jump from task to task, trying to do everything at once, and end up completing nothing at all.

One day, Joe's team was assigned a critical project that could potentially make or break the company. Joe, as usual, assured everyone that he would handle his part without a hitch. However, as the days passed, Joe found himself overwhelmed. He had volunteered for too many tasks, overestimating what he could handle in the time given.

The night before the project deadline, Joe sat in his cluttered office, surrounded by piles of unfinished work. The ticking clock seemed to mock him as he realized the gravity of the situation. His poor time management had not only put his job at risk but also the future of his company.

It was a wake-up call for Joe. He knew he had to change. He started by setting clear priorities and breaking down his tasks into manageable chunks. He learned to say no to additional responsibilities when his plate was already full. Slowly, Joe began to see a transformation. He was meeting deadlines, his stress levels dropped, and his colleagues started to rely on him again.

The story of Joe is a cautionary tale about the chaos that ensues when time is not managed wisely. It's a reminder that time is a finite resource and that managing it well can lead to not only professional success but also personal satisfaction and a well-balanced life.

Effective time management is transformative, serving as the rudder that steers the ship of daily life through calm and stormy seas alike. It instils a sense of purpose and direction, enabling individuals to navigate their days with confidence and clarity. By judiciously organizing tasks and commitments, one can avoid the tumult of last-minute rushes and the stress that accompanies them. This strategic approach to the day's hours fosters a harmonious balance between work and leisure, ensuring that deadlines are met without sacrificing the joys of personal pursuits. Moreover, it cultivates a disciplined mindset, which is instrumental in achieving long-term goals and aspirations. In essence, mastering the art of time management is akin to unlocking the full potential of one's life, allowing for a richer, more fulfilling existence. In today's fast-paced world, managing time effectively has become more crucial than ever. It's not just about squeezing more tasks into your day; it's about ensuring that you're focusing on the right things in the right way. Here's a guide to help you navigate the complexities of time management and emerge more productive and less stressed. Time management is the strategic allocation of your most valuable resource—time. It's about prioritizing tasks, setting goals, and finding an efficient way to achieve them. But remember, it's not a one-size-fits-all solution; it's a personalized strategy that fits your unique lifestyle and work rhythm.

Here are the detailed pillars of time management:

1. Prioritization

Prioritization is the foundation of effective time management. It involves evaluating tasks based on their urgency and importance. Prioritization is the strategic process of deciding the order and importance of tasks, ensuring that one's time and efforts are spent on the most significant activities. It is indeed the cornerstone of effective time management. At its core, prioritization is about making choices—often tough ones—about what to do, when to do it, and what not to do.

The Benefits of Prioritization

- **Focus:** Prioritization helps in maintaining focus on tasks that align with one's goals and values, reducing the time spent on less important activities.
- **Stress Reduction:** By managing tasks according to their importance, one can reduce the stress associated with overwhelming workloads.
- **Efficiency:** Prioritizing tasks allows for more efficient use of time, as it ensures that the most critical tasks are completed first.
- **Goal Achievement:** It aids in aligning daily tasks with long-term goals, making it more likely to achieve them.

Prioritization is a critical skill for effective time management, but it comes with its own set of challenges. Overcommitment is a common pitfall; when one takes on more tasks than they can handle, it becomes difficult to discern which tasks are truly important, leading to a diluted focus and reduced productivity. Procrastination is another significant hurdle; postponing essential tasks can create a backlog that not only hinders the prioritization process but also adds unnecessary stress and may lead to missed deadlines. Lastly, the challenge of distractions cannot be overstated. In an era where information overload is the norm, staying concentrated on the tasks at hand requires considerable discipline and effort. The ability to overcome these challenges is what distinguishes successful prioritization and, by extension, successful time management.

The Eisenhower Matrix is a popular tool for this, dividing tasks into four categories:

- Urgent and important (tasks you will do immediately).
- Important, but not urgent (tasks you will schedule to do later).
- Urgent, but not important (tasks you will delegate to someone else).
- Neither urgent nor important (tasks you will eliminate).

Apart from this there are two other popular tools:

- The ABCDE Method: A technique where tasks are assigned letters based on their significance, with 'A' being the most important and 'E' the least.
- The Ivy Lee Method: A simple strategy where one identifies the six most important tasks for the next day and focuses solely on completing them in order.

2. Planning

Planning is about mapping out your tasks and responsibilities. This can be done daily, weekly, or monthly. Effective planning involves:

- Setting goals: Define what you want to achieve in a specific period.
- Allocating time: Assign realistic time blocks to each task.
- Using tools: Utilize calendars, planners, and apps to keep track of your plans.

3. Execution

Execution is putting your plan into action. It requires discipline and focus. Key aspects include:

- Avoiding multitasking: Focus on one task at a time for better quality and efficiency.
- Minimizing distractions: Create a work environment that helps you stay focused.
- Staying flexible: Be prepared to adjust your plan as needed.

4. Reflection

Reflection involves looking back at what you've accomplished and what didn't go as planned. Reflective practices include:

- Reviewing your day: Take note of completed tasks and any interruptions.

- Analysing performance: Determine if you met your goals and where you can improve.
- Adjusting strategies: Modify your approach based on your analysis.

5. Balance

Balance is the goal of time management. It's about finding the right mix between work, personal life, and rest. Achieving balance involves:

- Setting boundaries: Know when to work and when to take a break.
- Taking care of yourself: Ensure you get enough rest, exercise, and leisure time.
- Being mindful: Stay present in the moment, whether you're working or relaxing.

By building your time management strategy around these pillars, you can create a more structured and less stressful life. It's a continuous process that requires commitment and regular refinement, but the benefits to your productivity and well-being are well worth the effort. It's about recognizing that not all tasks are created equal and that some activities will contribute more significantly to our goals and overall productivity than others.

Strategies for Effective Time Management

In today's fast-paced world, managing time effectively has become more crucial than ever. It's not just about squeezing more tasks into your day but about working smarter and not harder. Here are some simple and easy-to-implement strategies that can help you take control of your time and increase your productivity.

1. Plan Your Day: Start each day with a clear idea of what you need to accomplish. Make a to-do list the night before or first thing in the morning. This simple act sets a purposeful tone for the day.

2. Prioritize Tasks: Not all tasks are created equal. Use the Eisenhower Matrix to categorize tasks by urgency and importance, focusing on what truly moves the needle.

3. Break Down Projects: Large projects can be daunting. Break them into smaller tasks that are more manageable and less overwhelming. This makes it easier to start and maintain momentum.

4. Set Realistic Goals: Setting goals is essential, but they must be achievable. Unrealistic goals can lead to frustration and procrastination.

5. Eliminate Distractions: Identify what commonly distracts you in your work environment and take steps to minimize these interruptions. This might mean turning off notifications or setting boundaries with colleagues.

6. Learn to Say No: You can't do everything. Learn to decline requests that do not align with your priorities or that you do not have the bandwidth for.

7. Use Technology Wisely: Leverage apps and tools that can help you stay organized and track your time. Just be sure they don't become a distraction themselves.

8. Take Breaks: Short breaks throughout the day can improve focus and productivity. The Pomodoro Technique is a popular method that involves working for 25 minutes and then taking a 5-minute break.

9. Reflect on Your Day: At the end of each day, spend a few minutes reflecting on what you accomplished and what could be improved. This can help you plan better for the next day.

10. Continuous Improvement: Time management is a skill that can always be refined. Stay open to new strategies and be willing to adjust your approach as needed.

By implementing these strategies, you can start to take control of your time and make room for the things that matter most. Remember, effective time management is about quality, not just quantity. It's about making the most of the time you have and ensuring that your work aligns with your personal and professional goals. These strategies are a synthesis of various techniques and best practices found in the field of time management. For more detailed approaches and advanced techniques, consider exploring resources like Upwork's article on time management strategies, Better Up's guide to regaining control over your time, and Clockify's compilation of time management techniques. Each resource offers a unique perspective and additional tips that can further enhance your ability to manage time effectively.

The Clock and the Compass: In the bustling town of Ticktock, there lived a Clock and a Compass, both prized possessions of a young entrepreneur named Elara. The Clock, with its precise hands and unyielding tick, was a symbol of time's relentless march. The Compass, with its steadfast needle, represented direction and purpose.

Elara was a hardworking individual, but she often found herself overwhelmed by the demands of her growing business. The Clock would chime every hour, reminding her of the relentless passage of time, while the Compass lay silent, its needle pointing steadily north.

One evening, as the Clock struck midnight, Elara sat at her desk, surrounded by piles of paperwork, feeling the weight of unmet deadlines. The Compass, noticing her distress, spoke for the first time, "Why do you let the Clock dictate your life?"

Startled, Elara replied, "Because time is what I need the most and what I have the least."

The Compass gently spun its needle and said, "Time is infinite, but your energy is not. You must manage your time by prioritizing what truly matters. Let me guide you."

From that day forward, Elara used the Compass to find her true north. She learned to focus on tasks that aligned with her goals and values, rather than trying to chase every tick of the Clock. She discovered that by managing her time with intention, she could achieve balance and fulfilment.

The Clock continued to tick, but Elara no longer felt ruled by it. Instead, she danced to the rhythm of her own priorities, guided by the Compass, and her life was all the better for it.

This story illustrates the importance of prioritizing tasks and managing time effectively. It's not just about doing things right but doing the right things. Like Elara, we can use our 'compass' to navigate through life's demands, ensuring that we focus on what truly matters to us.

Balancing Work and Life

Balancing work and life are akin to walking a tightrope, where time management serves as the balancing pole that keeps us steady. It's about prioritizing tasks effectively, setting realistic goals, and carving out segments of time for different aspects of life. By managing time wisely, one can allocate hours for professional responsibilities while preserving moments for personal pursuits and relaxation. It involves recognizing that work is a part of life, not its entirety. This equilibrium is achieved through disciplined scheduling, understanding when to say no, and embracing the power of delegation. Ultimately, it's the art of making time work for you, not against you, allowing for a harmonious blend of productivity and personal fulfilment. In today's fast-paced world, mastering this balance is not just desirable, it's essential for maintaining mental well-being and nurturing relationships outside the workplace.

Overcoming Time Management Challenges

In the fast-paced world we live in, overcoming time management challenges is akin to mastering an art form. It requires a blend of self-awareness, planning, and discipline. To surmount these challenges, one must first acknowledge the finite nature of time and the importance of prioritizing tasks that align with personal and professional goals. Effective time management is about making intentional choices, which means saying no to non-essential tasks and yes to those that bring us closer to our aspirations. It involves setting clear, achievable goals and breaking them down into smaller, manageable tasks. Employing tools and techniques such as the Eisenhower Matrix or the Pomodoro Technique can help in categorizing tasks and maintaining focus. Moreover, reflection at the end of each day or week provides insights into what strategies worked and what didn't, allowing for continuous improvement in managing one's time. Ultimately, overcoming time management challenges empowers individuals to lead more productive, fulfilling lives.

In conclusion, mastering the art of time management is a journey that requires dedication, self-awareness, and continuous improvement. It's about finding a harmonious balance between your professional obligations, personal interests, and restorative downtime. As we navigate through the complexities of our daily lives, it becomes evident that managing time is not solely about efficiency and productivity; it's also about cultivating a lifestyle that values balance and moderation. By prioritizing tasks, setting realistic goals, and embracing flexibility, we can transform our relationship with time from one of scarcity to abundance. Let us carry forward the lessons learned in this chapter to create a more structured, purposeful, and fulfilling life. Remember, time is the canvas on which we paint our lives; let's make it a masterpiece.

TIME IS THE CANVAS; PRIORITIES ARE THE BRUSHSTROKES;
BALANCE IS THE MASTERPIECE.

Chapter 10: Inner Journey

Spiritual beliefs, practices, and connection with something greater than yourself

In the quiet corners of our hearts, beyond the mundane and the tangible, lies a yearning—an ancient whisper that beckons us to explore the depths of existence. This yearning is the essence of spirituality. It transcends religious dogmas, cultural boundaries, and the limitations of our senses. So, what exactly is spirituality, and why does it matter? Spirituality is a multifaceted concept that transcends the boundaries of religion and science. It encompasses our beliefs about the universe, our connection to others, and the mysteries of existence. While spirituality is deeply personal, its effects on health and well-being are increasingly recognized and studied.

Defining Spirituality

Spirituality is the broad concept of a belief in something beyond the self. It reaches beyond the material world, inviting us to ponder questions that defy easy answers: What is the meaning of life? How are we connected to each other? What truths lie hidden in the vast expanse of the universe? Spirituality is the profound belief in something beyond the self. It seeks to answer questions about life's purpose, suffering, and the interconnectedness of all beings. Whether rooted in religious traditions or a holistic sense of connection, spirituality provides a lens through which we perceive the world.

Unlike religion, which often adheres to structured doctrines, spirituality is more fluid. It's the dance of the soul—a quest for meaning, purpose, and connection. Let's explore its facets.

Signs of Spirituality

Spirituality manifests differently for each seeker. Here are some signs that you might be on a spiritual journey:

- Deep Questions: You find yourself pondering the nature of suffering, the afterlife, and the mysteries of existence. Spiritual seekers ponder existential questions, seeking meaning and purpose.
- Connection: You feel a deepening bond with other people, recognizing their shared humanity.
- Compassion and Empathy: Your heart expands, allowing you to feel the pain and joy of others. Spirituality fosters empathy, compassion, and interconnectedness with fellow humans.
- Interconnectedness: You sense that everything— trees, stars, animals, and humans—is woven together in a cosmic tapestry.
- Awe and Wonder: The sunrise, a newborn's smile, or the vastness of the night sky leaves you

breathless. Moments of awe—whether in nature or art—deepen spiritual experiences.

- Transcending Materialism: You seek happiness beyond possessions, and external rewards, understanding that fulfilment lies elsewhere.
- Quest for Meaning: You yearn to uncover the purpose behind your existence. A quest to contribute positively to the world.
- Desire for Impact: Making the world better becomes your mission.

Remember, spirituality isn't confined to temples or meditation cushions. It can bloom in a bustling city or a serene forest, during a heartfelt conversation or a solitary walk.

Types of Spirituality

Spirituality wears many robes. Let's explore a few based on the different types of practices:

- Breathwork: The rhythm of your breath becomes a gateway to the divine.
- Meditation: Silence becomes your sanctuary, and inner exploration your compass.
- New Age Spirituality: Crystals, energy healing, and chakras—embracing the mystical.
- Prayer: Whether whispered or shouted, it's a conversation with the cosmos.
- Service: Acts of kindness ripple through the universe.

- Nature Connection: The rustle of leaves, the scent of earth—nature as your temple.
- Spiritual Retreats: Sacred pauses to recharge and realign.
- Yoga: The union of body, mind, and spirit.

Spirituality can also to categorized based on the various belief systems:

- **Traditional Spirituality:** Rooted in established religious traditions such as Christianity, Islam, or Hinduism. It involves following rituals, scriptures, and teachings from these faiths.
- **Metaphysical Spirituality:** This type focuses on connecting to a higher consciousness within ourselves or to universal energy. It explores concepts like intuition, energy healing, and the interconnectedness of all things.
- **Humanistic Spirituality:** Humanists seek meaning and purpose through human experience, relationships, and personal growth. It emphasizes empathy, compassion, and interconnectedness with others.
- **Philosophical Spirituality:** Rooted in philosophical inquiry, this type explores questions about existence, morality, and the nature of reality. It doesn't necessarily involve religious practices but delves into deep philosophical concepts.
- **Body-Based Spirituality:** This approach recognizes the body-mind connection. Practices

like yoga, tai chi, and breathwork help individuals connect with their bodies, emotions, and inner wisdom.

- **Indigenous Spirituality:** Indigenous cultures worldwide have unique spiritual practices tied to their land, ancestors, and natural elements. These traditions emphasize harmony with nature and community.
- **Spiritualism:** Spiritualists believe in communication with spirits of the deceased. They often participate in séances, mediumship, and other practices to connect with the spirit world.

Benefits of Spirituality

Why embark on this mystical journey? Research suggests that those who embrace spirituality experience numerous health and well-being benefits. Reduced stress improved mental health, and a sense of purpose are just a few.

Whether you're religious, agnostic, or somewhere in between, incorporating simple spiritual practices into your routine can bring a sense of peace, purpose, and well-being. Let's explore some everyday practices that can help you tap into your inner wisdom and cultivate a deeper connection with yourself and the world around you.

1. Morning Meditation or Prayer

Starting your day with a short meditation or prayer sets a positive tone for the hours ahead. Take a few minutes to sit quietly, focus on your breath, and centre yourself. Whether you recite a prayer, practice mindfulness, or listen to a guided meditation, this morning ritual can ground you and align your intentions with your spiritual values.

2. Walking Meditation

Spiritual practice need not be confined to temples or complex rituals. A purposeful walk can also become a spiritual journey. As you walk, pay attention to each step, the rhythm of your breath, and the sensations in your body. Reflect on gratitude, release stress, and connect with the natural world around you. Walking mindfully can be a moving meditation that brings clarity and peace.

3. Daily Reflection

Set aside a few minutes each day for introspection. Reflect on your experiences, emotions, and thoughts. What did you learn? What challenges did you face? What moments brought you joy? Daily reflection helps you gain insights, make conscious choices, and appreciate the small blessings in life.

4. Mindfulness in Action

Mindfulness isn't just about sitting cross-legged; it's about being present in every moment. Whether you're washing dishes, sipping tea, or walking to work, practice mindfulness. Engage fully in the task at hand, noticing the details and sensations. By doing so, you infuse ordinary actions with spiritual awareness.

5. Follow Your Inner Voice

Listen to your intuition—the quiet whispers of your soul. Sometimes, our inner guidance speaks softly, nudging us toward certain decisions or actions. Trust these instincts. They often lead us toward alignment with our higher purpose.

6. Live with Intention

Set intentions for your day, week, or month. What do you want to create? How do you want to show up in the world? Living intentionally means aligning your actions with your values and aspirations.

7. Practice Compassion

Extend kindness to others and yourself. Compassion is a spiritual practice that fosters empathy, forgiveness, and understanding. When you treat others with compassion, you create a ripple effect of positive energy.

8. Let Go of the Past

Spirituality invites us to release old wounds, regrets, and grudges. Forgiveness—whether toward others or ourselves—frees us from emotional baggage. Embrace the present moment by unburdening your heart.

9. Connect with Nature

Step outside, breathe in fresh air, and observe the beauty around you. Nature has a way of grounding us and reminding us of our interconnectedness. Whether it's a tree, a flower, or a starry sky, find solace in the natural world.

10. Gratitude Practice

End your day by expressing gratitude. Reflect on the blessings, no matter how small. Write them down or simply say them aloud. Gratitude shifts our focus from what's lacking to what's abundant.

Remember, spirituality is a personal journey. Explore different practices, adapt them to your preferences, and allow them to evolve over time. The path to spiritual fulfilment is unique for each of us, but these simple practices can serve as stepping stones toward a more meaningful and centred life. So, take a deep breath, honour your spirit, and embrace the simplicity of these practices. Nourish your soul every day.

> **A Young Man and His Three Questions:** A young man troubled by his faith sought answers from a wise, old man. He posed three questions:
> "If God exists, why has no one seen Him?"
> "What is my destiny?"
> "How can the devil, born from fire, suffer in a hell made of fire?"
> The wise man smiled and slapped the young man gently. Surprised, the young man asked if he had offended the sage. The wise man explained: "Just as you feel pain

without seeing it, belief in God works similarly. Destiny matters less than how you handle it. And the devil's suffering is beyond mere physical elements." The young man left with newfound understanding: "Just because you don't see God doesn't mean He isn't there."

The Kind Villager: In a peaceful village, lived a man known for his kindness lived. His neighbours admired him, considering him the happiest person. Curious, another villager sought answers from this contented soul. Why was he so at peace? The kind villager shared: "I choose happiness. My positive outlook influences those around me. I am like an angel watching over everyone."
The lesson: Our attitude and kindness can create a little heaven around us.

Have you ever felt like there's something bigger out there, something beyond our everyday lives? That's what we call a spiritual connection. It's like feeling part of a huge family that includes everything in the universe.

- **We're All in This Together:** Imagine the universe as a giant puzzle, and each of us is one piece. Alone, a puzzle piece doesn't show much, but when all pieces come together, they create a beautiful picture. That's how we are connected to everything else—each person, tree, and star is part of a bigger picture.

- **Listening to the Universe's Whisper:** Sometimes, when it's quiet, and we're really listening, we can feel this connection. It might be while looking at the stars, hearing the ocean, or even feeling the wind on our face. These moments remind us that we're not alone; we're part of something huge and wonderful.

- **Finding the Connection Inside You:** To really feel this connection, we need to look inside ourselves. It's like going on an adventure inside your own heart. By thinking deeply, maybe through prayer or meditation, we can find a spark inside us that feels right and good. This spark is our personal link to the bigger world.

- **Embracing the Big Picture:** When we realize that we're a small part of a huge universe, it's like getting a big, warm hug from the world. We start to see that everything is connected, and we're just one of the many important parts.

- **Feeling at Peace with Your Place in the World:** This connection gives us a peaceful feeling. It's like knowing you're in the right place, doing what you're meant to do. Everything just feels like it fits together perfectly.

- **Being Called to Do Good Things:** This isn't just about feeling good; it's also about doing good. When we feel connected to the world, we want to take care of it. We might help others, protect nature, or just try to make the world a better place. It's our way of saying thank you for being part of something amazing.

Finding a connection with something greater than ourselves is like going on a never-ending journey. It's about discovering who we are and how we fit into the big, beautiful world around us. It's a journey that can make us feel happy, peaceful, and ready to spread goodness wherever we go.

In the final analysis, "Spirituality and Inner Journey" is a profound exploration of the self that transcends the materialistic confines of our existence. It's a quest for deeper understanding, a pursuit of inner peace, and a commitment to personal growth. As we close this chapter, let us reflect on the essence of spirituality as not just a concept but a practical guide to living. It's about nurturing our spiritual intelligence, enriching our lives with purpose, and fostering a sense of connectedness with the world around us. May this journey inspire us to embrace our true selves, cultivate compassion, and seek harmony within the tapestry of life. Let this be a reminder that our spiritual path is one of continual discovery, where each step taken in mindfulness brings us closer to the ultimate destination of self-realization and enlightenment.

SPIRITUALITY IS A UNIQUE JOURNEY,
WOVEN BY OUR SEEKING HEARTS.

Chapter 11. Personal Growth and Transformation

Personal evolution, learning, and the journey towards becoming your best self

Personal growth and transformation are not mere buzzwords; they represent profound journeys that shape our lives. As we traverse the winding roads of existence, we encounter moments of self-discovery, resilience, and evolution. In this blog, we delve into the essence of personal growth and explore how transformational experiences propel us towards self-actualization.

Personal growth and transformation are essential aspects of living a fulfilling and meaningful life. They involve changing your thoughts, behaviours, and beliefs to expand your consciousness and reach your highest potential. Personal growth and transformation are the processes of changing your thoughts, behaviours, and beliefs to expand your consciousness and live a more fulfilling life. They are not linear or static, but dynamic and ongoing. They can be intentional or spontaneous, internal or external, gradual or sudden. Personal growth entails expanding one's knowledge, skills, and capabilities, while transformation involves fundamental changes in one's attitudes, beliefs, and behaviours. It is through this continuous process that individuals evolve, adapt, and thrive in an ever-changing world.

Personal growth and transformation are important because they help you:

- Discover your true self and purpose
- Develop your strengths and talents
- Enhance your skills and knowledge
- Improve your health and well-being
- Increase your happiness and satisfaction
- Achieve your goals and dreams
- Contribute to the world and make a positive impact

Personal growth and transformation are not easy or comfortable. They require courage, commitment, and effort. They also involve facing your fears, overcoming your challenges, and learning from your failures. However, the rewards are worth it. You will become a better, wiser, and happier person.

Understanding Personal Growth: Our Greenhouse of Possibilities

The Seedlings of Self-Improvement

Picture this: You're tending your mental garden, planting seeds of curiosity, resilience, and newfound skills. Personal growth is like that—nurturing our minds, one metaphorical watering can at a time. Whether you're learning a new language, mastering the art of baking sourdough, or finally figuring out how to fold fitted sheets (seriously, it's an art!), each tiny step counts.

Authenticity: The Sunlight That Nourishes Us

Authenticity is our secret sauce. It's about embracing our quirks, celebrating our imperfections, and dancing like nobody's watching (even if your dance moves resemble a caffeinated chicken). When we show up as our genuine selves, we create space for growth. So go ahead, wear mismatched socks, belt out off-key tunes in the shower, and let your inner unicorn shine.

The Essence of Transformation: More Than Just a New Hairdo

Butterfly Mode: Engage!

Transformation isn't about superficial changes. It's not just swapping out your hairstyle or updating your wardrobe (although a fresh haircut does wonders!). It's about profound shifts—the kind that make caterpillars go, "Whoa, I'm a butterfly now!" Imagine shedding old beliefs, spreading your wings, and fluttering toward the sun. It's like a cosmic makeover, minus the cosmic contouring.

Dream Weaving: Crafting Extraordinary Futures

Personal growth builds upon what's already there, like adding layers to a cake. But transformation? Ah, that's where the magic happens. It's the blank canvas where you unleash your inner Picasso. Maybe you're switching careers, discovering your spiritual side, or deciding to become a professional llama whisperer (hey, it's a thing). Transformation births extraordinary futures—ones that make the universe raise an eyebrow and say, "Well, hello there!"

The first step is to cultivate self-awareness, the key to transformation. Self-awareness is the ability to recognize and understand your thoughts, feelings, motivations, and actions. It is also the ability to reflect on how they affect yourself and others. Let us grow through the few strategies to cultivate self-awareness:

- Keep a journal. In the quiet corners of our lives, where ink meets paper, lies a potent tool for self-discovery and transformation: the journal. Whether it's a leather-bound notebook or a digital app, journaling offers a sanctuary for our thoughts, emotions, and aspirations. Let's explore why keeping a journal matters and how it can enrich our lives.
  - Clarity Amid Chaos: Life often resembles a bustling marketplace, with thoughts and feelings jostling for attention. Journaling

provides a refuge—a space to untangle the threads of our minds. When we write down our experiences, fears, and hopes, we gain clarity. The act of putting words to our inner chaos helps us understand ourselves better. It's like turning on a light in a dim room; suddenly, everything becomes clearer.

- Processing Emotions: Emotions are like wild horses—they gallop through our hearts, sometimes trampling reason. By journaling, we tame these emotional steeds. We give them names, describe their colours, and trace their origins. As we write about joy, sorrow, anger, or love, we process them. We acknowledge their presence without judgment. Gradually, emotions lose their chaotic power and become companions on our journey.
- Tracking Progress: Imagine hiking up a mountain without markers. How would you know if you're getting closer to the summit? Journaling acts as those markers. We record our achievements, setbacks, and milestones. It's not just about big wins; even the small victories matter. Did you conquer a fear? Did you finish that book you've been meaning to read? Celebrate them all. These entries become stepping stones, guiding us forward.

o Noticing Patterns: Our lives follow patterns—seasons of growth, cycles of struggle. Journaling reveals these recurring themes. Maybe you notice that stress spikes during certain months or that creativity blooms after morning walks. By recognizing patterns, we gain insight. We can adjust our sails, anticipating storms or harnessing favourable winds. The journal becomes our compass, pointing toward self-improvement.

o Prompts and Possibilities: A blank page can be intimidating, but prompts come to the rescue. They nudge us gently: "Write about a moment of gratitude." "Describe a challenge you overcame." "List your dreams." These prompts spark creativity and prevent writer's block. And remember, there are no rules. You can scribble, draw, or spill your heart out. It's your canvas; paint it with authenticity.

o Gratitude and Goals: Gratitude journals are like sunflowers—they turn toward the light. When we jot down moments of gratitude, we cultivate joy. Similarly, writing about our goals fuels motivation. The journal becomes a garden where dreams take root. As we revisit old entries, we witness growth—the sapling becoming a sturdy tree.

- In the quiet hours before dawn or during a stolen lunch break, let your pen dance across the pages. Capture your essence—the messy, beautiful, evolving you. Your journal is a faithful companion, never judging, always listening. So, embrace this ancient practice. Write about sunsets, heartaches, and whispered dreams. In doing so, you'll find not just words but fragments of your soul.

- Meditate. In the cacophony of modern existence, where notifications clamour for our attention and stress weaves a tight web, meditation emerges as an oasis—a quiet refuge where the mind can find solace. This ancient practice, once confined to Himalayan caves, now graces our bustling lives, offering profound benefits that ripple through our mental and physical well-being.

  - The Breath, Our Anchor: At the heart of meditation lies simplicity: the breath. We turn our gaze inward, observing each inhale and exhale. As thoughts flutter like restless birds, we gently guide them back to this rhythmic anchor. In this dance of attention, we discover a sanctuary—a place where the mind can rest, unburdened by the past or anxious about the future.

  - A Symphony of Mantras and Objects: Meditation wears many robes. Some chant mantras, sacred syllables that resonate within. Others fix their gaze on a flickering candle or a serene image. The object becomes a portal, leading us beyond the mundane. Whether it's the hum of "Om" or the texture of a stone, these focal points invite us to presence.

- o Calm Waters, Relaxed Shores: As we sit in stillness, our nervous system receives a memo: "It's safe." Cortisol—the stress hormone—takes a backseat. Our muscles unclench, shoulders easing their burden. Blood pressure softens, and the heart beats in sync with the universe. The body, like a taut bow, finds release.
- o The Mind's Canvas, Awareness: Meditation sharpens our inner lens. We witness thoughts parading by—the mundane and the profound, the whispers of worry and the echoes of joy. Instead of chasing them, we observe. Like a painter stepping back from the canvas, we gain perspective. Awareness blooms—a lotus in the mud.
- o Guided Paths and Digital Sanctuaries: Ten minutes a day—that's all it takes. Guided meditations, like gentle hands, lead us through forests of tranquillity. Apps whisper mantras into our ears, and music cradles our consciousness. We explore mindfulness, compassion, and loving-kindness. The digital age bows to ancient wisdom.

- o The Ripple Effect: Meditation isn't a solitary affair. Its tendrils touch every facet of life. Anxiety, once a tempest, now a gentle breeze. Sleep, a velvet cloak. Concentration, a sharpened arrow. And compassion? It spills from our hearts, irrigating parched souls. We become architects of our inner landscape.
  - o The Invitation: So, find a quiet corner—a cushion, a park bench, or the edge of your bed. Close your eyes. Breathe. Let thoughts drift like autumn leaves. Ten minutes—a gift to yourself. In this sacred pause, you'll discover that the universe resides within—a vast, silent expanse waiting to be explored.
  - o Remember, dear seeker, meditation isn't about escaping life; it's about diving deeper.
- Seek feedback. In the vast tapestry of personal growth, feedback emerges as a guiding constellation—a celestial map that illuminates our blind spots and propels us toward excellence. Let us delve into the art of seeking feedback, for within its folds lie wisdom, evolution, and the promise of becoming our best selves.
  - o The Echo Beyond Self-Perception: We are like actors on a stage, performing our roles with fervour. Yet, our view is limited—a spotlight that casts shadows. Feedback extends the stage, revealing the audience's perspective. It whispers, "Here's what you don't see." Whether it's a standing ovation

or a gentle critique, it expands our self-awareness.

- o The Alchemy of Mistakes: Mistakes—those humble stepping stones—are often our greatest teachers. Feedback transforms them from stumbling blocks into alchemical ingredients. When someone points out a misstep, they offer a recipe for growth. We mix humility with curiosity, stir in reflection, and bake resilience. Voilà! A golden lesson emerges.
- o Mirrors Held by Others: Friends, family, colleagues—they wield mirrors. Their reflections reveal facets we overlook—the way we communicate, our body language, the impact of our words. Like a sculptor shaping clay, we adjust. Perhaps we soften our tone or stand taller. Feedback becomes our chisel, carving a truer likeness.
- o Mentors: The Lighthouses: Mentors—wise souls who've weathered storms—guide us. They share their compasses, pointing toward uncharted waters. Their feedback isn't just about technique; it's about character. "Listen," they say, "your sails need trimming." We adjust, grateful for their candour. Their legacy becomes our compass rose.
- o Coaches: Architects of Mastery: Coaches, like architects, blueprint our skills. They watch our game—the swing of a tennis

racket, the brushstroke on canvas. Their feedback isn't sugar-coated; it's the mortar that strengthens our foundation. "Shift your weight," they advise. We recalibrate, inching toward mastery.

- Surveys and Quizzes: The Silent Witnesses: Surveys and quizzes—silent observers—gather data. They're like cosmic dust, settling on our journey. Did the workshop resonate? Was the presentation stellar or lacklustre? Their questions echo across time. We analyse patterns, tweak our orbits, and chart new trajectories.
- The Art of Receiving: Feedback isn't a monologue; it's a duet. When it knocks, we open the door. We listen—not defensively but curiously. We thank the messenger, even if their words sting. Like a sculptor who honours the stone, we honour their intent. And when we act on their insights, we harmonize.
- The Dance of Growth: Imagine a waltz with feedback—the rise and fall, the twirls of improvement. We stumble, but the rhythm pulls us up. We learn to pirouette on criticism's edge, transforming it into grace. The dance isn't linear; it's a spiral—a galaxy of iterations.
- So, dear seeker of constellations, seek feedback. From the applause of friends to the critique of mentors, gather stardust.

- Try new things. Life, like an unexplored canvas, invites us to dip our brushes into vibrant hues and create our own masterpiece. Amid the familiar strokes, there lies a thrilling invitation: to try new things. Let us unfurl this parchment of curiosity and discover the magic that awaits.

    o The Alchemy of Discovery: Imagine a treasure chest hidden in the attic of your existence. Each new endeavour is a key—a chance to unlock its secrets. Whether it's strumming a guitar, learning a dance form, or baking a soufflé, you unravel hidden facets of yourself. The thrill lies not only in the outcome but in the journey—the notes fumbled, the flour dusted, the feet tripped. These are the brushstrokes that colour your soul.

    o Challenging Assumptions: Assumptions are like well-worn paths—the ones we tread without questioning. Trying new things disrupts this inertia. It whispers, "What if?" What if you, the introvert, tried stand-up comedy? What if the spreadsheet wizard dabbled in watercolours? These leaps defy assumptions, revealing uncharted territories. Perhaps you'll find laughter or a masterpiece—or both.

    o The Expanding Horizon: Imagine your mind as a room with walls that inch closer each day. Trying new things is like opening a window. Suddenly, the horizon stretches—

an endless savanna of possibilities. A language course introduces you to new syntax; a solo trip reveals the poetry of solitude. Your mental landscape broadens, and you become a citizen of the world.

- o Hobbies: The Kaleidoscope of Joy: Hobbies are like secret gardens. You plant seeds—knitting needles, chess pieces, bonsai saplings—and watch them bloom. The gardener within you tends to these passions. Maybe you'll weave scarves, checkmate opponents, or sculpt miniature forests. Hobbies aren't just pastimes; they're portals to joy.
- o Courses: The Classroom of Curiosity: Enrol in a course—a vessel that sails through knowledge's seas. Perhaps it's astrophysics or calligraphy. As you sit in virtual or physical classrooms, you sip from the cup of curiosity. The equations align, the ink flows, and suddenly, your part of a cosmic conversation. Learning isn't confined to youth; it's a lifelong voyage.
- o Books: The Time-Traveling Companions: Books are doorways to epochs and galaxies. Fiction or nonfiction, they beckon. A novel transport you to Victorian London; a self-help book hands you a compass. You meet characters—kindred spirits or foes—and they whisper, "Come, explore." So, read—the pages rustle, and you journey.

- o Travel: The Nomad's Song: Travel isn't just about destinations; it's about becoming. The Eiffel Tower, the Himalayas, a bustling market in Marrakech—they're mirrors. You see yourself reflected—the awe, the fear, the wonder. Travel nudges you out of comfort zones, urging you to taste exotic spices, decipher foreign alphabets, and dance with the unknown.
  - o Styles, Roles, Perspectives: The Shape-Shifting Quest: Try on different hats—the poet's beret, the scientist's lab coat, the philosopher's cloak. Slip into roles—the listener, the leader, the learner. Change perspectives—see the world through a child's eyes or an elder's wisdom. These experiments aren't frivolous; they're portals to empathy and growth.
  - o So, dear adventurer, step beyond the threshold. The canvas awaits your strokes, the notes your fingers. Try new things—boldly, curiously. And remember, every beginning is a sunrise—a promise of magic.
- Be mindful. In the whirlwind of existence, where time races and screens glow, there exists a quiet sanctuary—the realm of mindfulness. It beckons us to step off the carousel, to breathe, and to witness life as it unfolds. Let us explore this ancient practice—a lantern in the labyrinth of modernity.
  - o The Stillness Within: Mindfulness isn't about escaping life's chaos; it's about

sinking into its depths. Imagine a pond—the ripples of thoughts and emotions disturb its surface. Mindfulness invites us to sit by this pond, watching the ripples settle. We become the silent witness—the lotus blooming amidst the mud.

o   The Breath, Our Anchor: Close your eyes. Feel the air glide across your nostrils—the cool inhale, the warm exhale. The breath is our anchor—the rhythm that tethers us to the present. When distractions pull us away—a buzzing phone, a racing mind—we return to the breath. Inhale. Exhale. Here. Now.

o   Body as Temple: Our bodies are vessels of sensation—the hum of blood, the touch of fabric, the weight of bones. Mindfulness invites us to inhabit this temple. Scan your body—the tightness in your shoulders, the pulse in your wrists. Befriend discomfort; it's a messenger. When we listen, it softens.

o   The Symphony of Senses: Mindfulness isn't just about the mind; it's a symphony of senses. Taste the warmth of tea, hear the rustle of leaves, see the play of light on water. Each sense is a portal—a way to step out of thought loops and into raw experience. The mundane becomes extraordinary.

o   Gratitude, the Magic Elixir: Gratitude is sunlight for the soul. When we pause and say, "Thank you," we sip from this elixir. Notice the small wonders—the steam rising from your cup, the laughter of a child, the curve of a petal. Gratitude shifts our lens; suddenly, life sparkles.

o   Affirmations, Seeds of Transformation: Words are spells—chants that shape reality. Affirmations are seeds we plant in the fertile soil of our minds. "I am enough." "I am resilient." Repeat them like mantras. Gradually, they take root. We blossom—a garden of self-love.

o   Visualization, Dreaming Awake: Close your eyes again. Imagine—a sunflower turning toward the sun, a mountain standing unwavering. Visualization isn't escapism; it's dreaming awake. Picture your goals— the book you'll write, the dance you'll master. The mind doesn't distinguish between real and imagined; it paints both on the canvas of possibility.

o   The Art of Non-Judgment: Thoughts parade through our minds—the critic, the worrier, the dreamer. Mindfulness doesn't judge; it observes. When negativity arises, we nod. "Ah, there you are." Like clouds passing across the sky, thoughts drift. We don't cling; we let them go.

o   The Gift of Presence: Mindfulness isn't a destination; it's the journey—the footprints in dew-kissed grass, the scent of rain. So,

pause. Look up at the sky—the cerulean expanse. Listen—the wind's whisper. Be here, fully. The present moment—the only place where life unfolds.
- o Remember, dear seeker, mindfulness isn't a task; it's a way of being. In each breath, each heartbeat, you touch eternity.

I used to be a very shy and introverted person during my school days. I had a hard time making friends, expressing.
, and taking risks. I was afraid of being judged, rejected, or ridiculed by others. I preferred to stay in my comfort zone and avoid any challenges or conflicts.

It was during my college days, I decided to change. I realized that I was missing out on a lot of opportunities and experiences because of my fear and insecurity. I wanted to grow as a person and discover new aspects of myself. I wanted to live a more fulfilling and meaningful life.

So, I started to take small steps to overcome my shyness and introversion. I joined a gang that matched my interests and hobbies. I participated in class discussions and college projects. I volunteered for a local charity organization. I signed up for a public speaking course. I tried to talk to new people and make friends.

It was not easy. I faced many challenges and setbacks along the way. I felt nervous, anxious, and awkward at times. I made mistakes and embarrassed myself. I faced criticism and rejection. But I did not give up. I learned from my failures and improved myself. I celebrated my successes and appreciated myself. I gained confidence and courage.

Gradually, I became a more outgoing and extroverted person. I developed new skills and abilities. I explored new passions and interests. I met new people and made new friends. I experienced new things and had new adventures. I became happier and more satisfied with myself and my life.

I am proud of myself for taking charge of my personal evolution and learning. I am grateful for the journey that I have taken and the person that I have become. I am still growing and learning every day, and I look forward to becoming my best self.

The Role of Self-Reflection: Self-reflection plays a pivotal role in personal growth and transformation. Taking the time to introspect, evaluate experiences, and learn from them allows us to identify areas for improvement. By examining our thoughts, emotions, and actions, we gain insights that lead to positive change. Whether it's overcoming challenges, developing resilience, or fostering empathy, self-reflection fuels our journey toward transformation.

Self-reflection acts as a catalyst for personal growth and transformation, enabling individuals to gain self-awareness, identify areas for improvement, and make intentional changes in their lives. By engaging in self-reflection, individuals embark on a journey of self-discovery, embracing their strengths and weaknesses, and uncovering their true potential. This process empowers individuals to learn from past experiences, make conscious choices, and continuously evolve, ultimately leading to personal growth and transformation.

The Role of Self-Reflection: Your Inner Mirror

Self-reflection acts as a catalyst for personal transformation by facilitating self-awareness, uncovering limiting beliefs, aligning actions with values, and embracing change. It empowers us to recognize and leverage our strengths, address our weaknesses, and set goals that align with our true selves. As we engage in self-reflection, we embark on a transformative journey—one that transcends mere growth and leads to profound shifts in our mindset, behaviour, and overall well-being. Here are some friendly steps to weave self-reflection into your routine:

- **Morning Musing:** Picture this—your favourite mug, a cozy corner, and a few minutes of quiet. Set a regular time in the morning to sip your coffee or tea and reflect. It's like a warm hug for your soul.
- **Nature Nook:** Find a spot outdoors—a park bench, a grassy patch, or even your balcony. Breathe in the

fresh air, listen to the birds, and let your thoughts wander. Nature has a way of inspiring reflection.

- **Tiny Windows:** You don't need an hour! Start small. Dedicate just a few minutes. Maybe while waiting for your toast to pop or during your commute. These tiny windows add up to big insights.
- **Question Time:** Use prompts to kickstart your reflections. Ask yourself:
    - What made me smile yesterday?
    - Did I learn something new?
    - How did I handle that little hiccup?
- **Journal Joy:** Grab a colourful notebook (or open a digital one). Jot down your musings. It's like having a heart-to-heart chat with yourself. Plus, doodles are encouraged!
- **Rewind and Replay:** At day's end, hit the mental rewind button. Reflect on your interactions, victories, and even those quirky moments. What surprised you? What can you celebrate?
- **Zen Zone:** Try mindfulness. Close your eyes, take a deep breath, and let thoughts drift by like clouds. No judgment, just observation. It's like a mental spa day.
- **High-Five Yourself:** Celebrate progress! Did you handle stress better today? Did you choose kindness? High-five!
- **Oops, I Learned:** Mistakes happen—they're like plot twists in your life story. Instead of beating yourself up, ask, "What's the lesson here?" It's like finding treasure in the mess.

- **You're Awesome:** Be kind to yourself. Imagine your inner cheerleader doing cartwheels. You're growing, evolving, and rocking this self-reflection thing!

It's not about perfection; it's about progress. So go ahead, sprinkle some self-reflection stardust into your days!

The Cha-Cha of Life

Life isn't a straight line; it's a cha-cha. We stumble, twirl, and occasionally step on our own toes. But guess what? Each stumble becomes a shimmy toward growth, and every twirl propels us toward self-actualization. So, let's embrace the messy, beautiful dance—the one that leaves stardust on our shoes and constellations in our hearts.

Remember, dear reader, the journey itself is the destination. So, keep evolving, keep transforming, and sprinkle kindness like confetti.

FOR EVERY STEP YOU TAKE IN LEARNING IS A LEAP TOWARDS BECOMING YOUR BEST SELF. REMEMBER, THE PATH TO GREATNESS ISN'T A SPRINT, IT'S A MARATHON.

Chapter 12. Conclusion

Legacy of excellence can be formed and passed down through generations

Leaving a positive legacy involves making a significant impact in your personal or professional life that will be remembered and appreciated by others. A "Legacy of Excellence" is a powerful concept that embodies the transmission of high standards, values, and achievements from one generation to the next. It is formed when individuals strive for excellence in their respective fields, be it in arts, sciences, sports, or any other domain, and their accomplishments become a benchmark for future generations. This pursuit of excellence is not confined to personal success; it also includes the positive impact made on society and the world at large. As this legacy is passed down, each generation is inspired to uphold these standards and even surpass them, thereby perpetuating a cycle of continuous improvement and achievement. This enduring legacy of excellence, therefore, serves as a guiding light, motivating and driving successive generations towards greater heights. It is a testament to the timeless nature of excellence and its capacity to inspire, influence, and shape the future.

Let's delve deeper into each of the steps:

Live by Your Values: Your values are the principles that give your life meaning, direction and purpose. It's important to identify these values and strive to live by them. For example, if you value honesty, then always speak the truth. If you value kindness, then make an effort to be kind to others. Living by your values is a way of being true to yourself and setting a positive example for others.

Make a Positive Impact: Making a positive impact means contributing to the well-being and success of others. This could be in your personal relationships, in your community, or in the wider world. For example, you could volunteer at a local charity, help a friend in need, or work on projects that benefit society. The key is to act with kindness and generosity, without expecting anything in return.

Pursue Excellence: Pursuing excellence means striving to be the best you can be in whatever you do. This could be in your career, your hobbies, or your personal life. It involves setting high standards for yourself and working hard to achieve them. Remember, excellence is not about being perfect; it's about continuous improvement and learning from your mistakes.

Educate and Inspire: Sharing your knowledge and experiences can have a profound impact on others. You could mentor a young person, teach a class, write a book, or simply share your wisdom with friends and family. By educating and inspiring others, you can help them to grow and succeed.

Take Care of the Environment: Our natural environment is a precious resource that we should strive to protect. This could involve recycling, reducing your carbon footprint, or supporting environmental causes. By taking care of the environment, you can leave a positive legacy for future generations.

Create Something Lasting: Creating something lasting could involve writing a book, starting a business, or building a house. It could also be something intangible, like a family tradition or a positive change in your community. The key is to create something that will continue to have a positive impact long after you're gone.

Remember, leaving a positive legacy is about more than just being remembered. It's about making a difference in the world and inspiring others to do the same. It's about living a life of purpose and meaning. So, think about what kind of legacy you want to leave, and start taking steps to make it a reality.

YOUR TRUE LEGACY IS ETCHED IN THE HEARTS AND MINDS OF THOSE
YOU TOUCH, NOT IN MONUMENTS OF STONE OR ACHIEVEMENTS ALONE.

www.ingramcontent.com/pod-product-compliance
Lightning Source LLC
LaVergne TN
LVHW010454200726
843506LV00002B/108